Forever Romances

Love Is the Key

IRENE B. BRAND

Forever Romances

is an imprint of
Guideposts Associates, Inc.
Carmel, NY 10512

Love Is the Key
Copyright © 1988 by Irene Brand

This Guideposts edition is published by special arrangement with
Ballantine Books, a Division of Random House.

ISBN 0-310-47801-4

Scripture quotations are taken from the *Holy Bible: New International
Version* (North American Edition), copyright © 1973, 1978, 1984, by the
International Bible Society, used by permission of Zondervan Bible
Publishers, and the King James Version.

Edited by Anne Severance and Sandra L. Vander Zicht
Designed by Kim Koning

Printed in the United States of America

To
Sharon, David, Sandra

chapter
1

"PLEASE DON'T GO THROUGH WITH THIS, ALISHA!" Holly Jameson begged as she fitted the lace wedding veil over her friend's short brown hair, styled in a careless windswept fashion.

Eyes glistening with tears, Alisha DeFoe lifted a shaking hand to bolster trembling lip, and shook her head. "It's too late now," she murmured. Through the walls of the little room where she waited with her maid-of-honor, Alisha could hear the strains of the pipe organ as the musician struck the opening chords of the nuptial music.

"It *will* be if you walk down that aisle!" Holly insisted. "Why don't you just duck out of here? You could hide for a few days, then go with our sorority group to Europe like you want to do."

Alisha smiled bitterly. "What do you think I'd do for money? Oh, my folks gave me a few traveler's checks to use for incidentals on my honeymoon," she admitted wearily, "but it's hardly enough for a summer vacation abroad."

A rumble sounded through the stone walls of Buffalo's Covenant Church, one of New York's most prestigious congregations, and Alisha peered out the window. No rain yet, but threatening clouds darkened the afternoon sun.

Mother arranged everything else. Why couldn't she have held off the rain for another hour?

"I've been wondering—" Alisha's best friend, lovely in mauve taffeta, picked up her bouquet of miniature carnations and baby's breath and pressed it to her nose. Inhaling the fragrant aroma, she lifted her head and looked directly into the dark blue eyes circled with fatigue and unhappiness. "—Why are your parents so determined that you marry your father's business partner, anyway?"

Alisha shrugged her small shoulders which seemed oddly overwhelmed by the elaborate wedding gown. "That's easy. He's rich, of course. Not to mention the fact that he's a member of an old-line family. Just the kind of man Mother has always wanted . . . for me."

Holly grimaced. "He's *also* your father's age."

"Not only that—" Alisha rose and stood inspecting her doleful countenance in the full-length mirror. "Lately I've had a hassle keeping him at arm's length. Tonight—" She gave an involuntary shudder of revulsion. "—Tonight I'll be Mrs. Theodore Blevins. Frankly, Holly, I'm terrified!" The look she turned on her friend was convincing.

The tall blonde was puzzled. "But this isn't the Victorian era. Marriages aren't arranged anymore. Whatever possessed you to agree to such a thing?"

"Someone as uninhibited and independent as you would never understand, Holly." Alisha lifted the huge bouquet of red roses and baby's breath from the florist's box, then held them as far away as possible. The scent was nauseating. She recalled the first flowers that Theodore had sent her, and her mother's words came back to her: *This is your chance, Alisha . . . our chance! If you marry Theodore Blevins, your father's success is assured!* She blinked. "Uh . . . Mother's so sure Theodore is right for me."

"But are *you* sure?"

There was a deep sadness in the soft voice. "What you don't know is that Mother had a very unhappy first marriage. She vowed that no daughter of hers would ever make the same mistake."

"But isn't it a mistake to marry a man you don't love?" Holly was pleading now. "And you don't love him . . . do you?"

Alisha looked out the leaded glass at the stormy sky. It looked as if it were going to rain, after all. "Mother says love will come later." Squaring her shoulders, she lifted her head and looked her friend in the eye. "Besides, I've made up my mind. I—I can't let my parents down now."

"Are you ready, my dear?" Alfred DeFoe tapped on the door. "It's time."

Holly reached over to give the bride a fierce hug before slipping from the room, past the portly man who waited in the hallway.

Alisha moved to meet her father on legs that refused to stop trembling, her face as white as the elegant gown she wore. "I'm . . . ready," she said resolutely.

In the foyer of the church she looked at her father, and yearned for the comfort he would not give her. The last time she had begged her parents to forget the wedding, he had refused to listen. "Alisha, you've been reading too many romantic novels. Blevins can lay the world at your feet, and he's foolish about you. Someday—if you're half as smart as I think you are—you'll thank us for arranging this marriage for you."

Someday, Alisha thought, *but not today.* She tried to still her thoughts, but her brain rampaged. With all too few opportunities to see a model family, she had still expected that her own home would be founded on love.

9

With measured strides, Holly reached her place at the front of the church and turned, just as the organist ended "Ode to Joy" and began the trumpet fanfare announcing the wedding march.

Alisha looked at the long aisle stretching ahead of her and felt the dizzying sensation of one who is standing on the brink of a precipice. The scene blurred as she took her first reluctant steps toward the man who waited at the altar banked with flowers. *This is wrong, wrong! If my parents really loved me, they wouldn't have asked me to do this.* Then, as if an accusing angel sat on her shoulder, she heard, *When your sister died, you gave up your right to a life of your own. Remember?*

Remember? She could never forget. Alisha shook her head slightly to erase the grim picture. Thoughts of Theodore were easier to take than thoughts of her sister's death.

As she drew nearer the altar, his face shifted into focus— the sagging eyelids screening gray eyes behind dark-rimmed glasses, the double chin drooping below his tight collar. His complexion was unusually florid today, she thought, noticing the bright red splotches high on his pudgy cheeks. *I wonder if he's having any last-minute regrets? Or,* and her heart sank at the prospect, *maybe he's thinking about the honeymoon. . . .*

The next step would bring her to his side. Soon she would be uttering the sacred vow, "'Till death do us part." Mechanically, she moved into place before the minister, separated briefly from her groom by her father's body.

The wedding march ended in a thunderous crescendo, and in its wake, an answering peal of thunder rang outside. Then, only silence. No one coughed. No one stirred in the pews. Alisha's pulse throbbed in her throat, and she wondered if the sound could be heard all over the building.

The lull before the storm, thought Alisha as the minister started the ceremony.

"Dearly beloved, we are gathered together in the sight of God, and in the presence of these witnesses, to join this man and this woman in holy matrimony. This honorable estate, instituted by God, was adorned and beautified by the presence of our Lord Jesus Christ at the marriage in Cana of Galilee. Therefore, marriage is not to be entered into by any unadvisedly, but reverently, discreetly, and in the love of God."

The minister's words struck Alisha like a cracking whip. She had never really listened to the wedding service before. Now the words fairly screamed at her. Marriage constituted a pact with God, as well as with the man so near her side. She had considered her mother's anger if she refused to marry Theodore, but not God's displeasure if she *did*.

"Who giveth this woman to be married to this man?"

Beneath the heavy veil, Alisha could feel tiny beads of moisture spring to her forehead.

"I do," said her father, stepping back and placing her hand in Theodore's clammy one.

This was the moment when she was to hand Holly her bouquet. She cast her friend a frantic look, and for one brief instant, their eyes locked. *Don't do it, Alisha! Don't do it!*

"I charge you both," intoned the minister, "as you stand in the presence of God, to remember that love and loyalty alone will avail as the foundation of a happy and enduring home. If the solemn vows which you are about to make be kept inviolate, and if steadfastly you seek to do the will of your heavenly Father, your life will be full of peace and joy, and the home which you are establishing will endure through every vicissitude."

If these were the conditions for peace and joy, theirs would be a miserable union, she moaned inwardly. Theodore's grip tightened, and she felt as if a key were being turned in a lock.

I can't do it! It's one thing to be a dutiful daughter, but that duty should stop short of sacrificing twenty-two years of virtuous living to a man I don't love. Had she waited too long? The minister was already reading the vows.

"Theodore Blevins, wilt thou have this woman to be thy wedded wife, to live together in the holy estate of matrimony? Wilt thou love her, comfort her, honor and keep her, in sickness and in health; and forsaking all others, keep thee only unto her, so long as ye both shall live?"

"I will," Theodore replied without hesitation.

Alisha's hand crept to her high collar and pulled at it with nervous fingers. Her palms were moist. She ran her tongue over her hot, dry lips. "Alisha DeFoe—" the minister addressed her, his voice grating on her taut nerves "— wilt thou have this man to be thy wedded husband, to live together in the holy estate of matrimony? Wilt thou love him, comfort him, honor and keep him, in sickness and in health; and forsaking all others, keep thee only unto him, so long as ye both shall live?"

In the breathless hush that followed, Alisha opened her mouth, but she could not force a single word past the enormous lump in her throat. How could her parents, who had always taught her the value of truthfulness, expect her to continue this charade? She pulled again at the collar of her dress. Seconds ticked by, and she sensed the dreadful silence in the church as the guests waited for her answer.

The minister cleared his throat and prompted, "'I will.'"

Alisha succeeded in swallowing and gazed at the minister with a clear eye. From somewhere deep within, a little spurt of courage budded and made its way to her tongue.

"But I *won't*," she said, her voice carrying clearly to the assembled wedding guests.

There was a collective gasp from the congregation, and in

the stunned silence that followed, Alisha heard her mother's strangled cry, "Alisha!"

She spoke softly at first, her words intended only for the wedding party. "I don't honor Theodore, nor do I love him. I consented to this wedding to please my parents, but not even for them will I make a mockery of marriage. If I took these vows, feeling as I do, it would be a terrible mistake. So, I'm very sorry, but . . . I won't."

Alisha glanced once at Theodore, a deep red suffusing his face, then she turned quickly and started down the aisle. In her flight she noted only two things—her mother's ashen face and Holly's bright smile of approval.

At the door, she picked up her billowing skirts, scampered down the steps of the church, and fled up the sidewalk. She ran for several blocks before the enormity of what she had done dawned on her.

"Now what?" she muttered aloud, pausing to catch her breath. "I can't run around town in a wedding gown. And I can't go home! Alisha DeFoe," she scolded, "you've done some pretty stupid things in your life, but this time, as far as Mother and Father are concerned, you've committed the unpardonable sin!"

Arriving at Broadway Avenue, Alisha turned a corner rather than cross the busy thoroughfare. To add to the trauma of the day, she felt the first drops of rain from the storm that had threatened all afternoon.

Zach Martin had just left a telephone booth and was crossing the sidewalk to his pickup truck when an unaccustomed sight greeted his eyes. He blinked, laughed at the spectacle, and whistled a few bars of "Here Comes the Bride."

His smile faded, however, when the young woman approached and he caught his first real glimpse of her. Though her features were drawn, he could see that she was a real beauty. Her hair, the rich, dark color of his favorite coffee, blew wildly about a face gone white as the gown she was wearing. But it was the startlingly blue eyes that captured and held his attention. He had never seen such pure misery in his life.

At first, Zach had assumed she was involved in some kind of advertising scheme. But this was no gimmick. The young woman was in trouble—serious trouble, from the looks of things.

As she drew nearer, her bundlesome skirt slipped out of her hand, her shoe caught in the fabric, and she stumbled and fell forward, arms outstretched in an effort to keep her balance. Acting instinctively, Zach stepped in front of her and cushioned the fall.

"Oh!" Alisha cried as strong arms encircled her waist.

"Steady, lady."

She looked up into laughing brown eyes. At that moment the rain descended, heavy pelting drops that threatened a deluge. Simultaneously, the tears that Alisha had suppressed all day brimmed over and spilled down her cheeks.

"Hold on, now, no tears! Isn't there enough water around here?" Zach held her a moment, enjoying the feel of the small form in his arms before setting her on her feet. *No woman has the right to look that dazzling when she cries,* he thought, drawing in his breath sharply. Slumbering feelings stirred dangerously. *Take it easy, old man. This isn't for you, and you know it.*

Alisha made a quick appraisal of her rescuer. He looked harmless enough. The tall man flashed an encouraging smile, displaying even, white teeth. The chiseled face was framed in a dark beard, and rumpled black hair fell forward over a high brow. Still, he was dressed in rough clothing—

Taking a chance, she plunged ahead. "My mother will never forgive me if I ruin this dress!" she began impulsively. The fragile fabric, growing heavier with the downpour, tugged at her throat, and the wisp of veil wilted completely. She removed the coronet of lace and seed pearls and tucked it under one arm, pushing back her damp hair with a trembling hand. "I'm embarrassed to ask a stranger, but I don't have any money with me. Could you . . . that is, would you . . . lend me money for taxi fare?"

The man looked genuinely sympathetic. "Since there isn't a taxi in sight and since my truck is parked right here, why don't you let me drive you . . . wherever it is you were going."

"But I wouldn't want to impose." She began a mild protest. "Besides, I don't know you."

The smile was exchanged for a full, deep-throated chuckle. "You probably wouldn't know the taxi driver, either. Come on, before you're completely soaked." He urged her toward the blue truck parked at the curb.

Alisha felt herself being lifted to the high seat, her voluminous skirts and train tucked about her. Then, without another word, the man slammed the door and sprinted to the driver's side. The engine purred to life at the turn of a key, and the wipers cleared the broad windshield.

Within the confines of the vehicle, Alisha gave the man a sidelong glance, observing his impressive height. His wavy hair brushed the top of the cab, and she felt strangely reassured by his solid presence.

"Where to, lady?"

"Home . . . I guess," she said hesitantly, then leaned forward to inspect the street signs. "Drive east on Broadway until you come to the interstate, then south to West Seneca."

They drove in silence for a few blocks. Zach figured someone dressed for a wedding needed time to compose herself. Not that he wasn't curious, but "curiosity killed the cat," or so Gran had told him a long time ago. Once the young woman looked his way, as if wondering whether she could trust him. He kept his eyes on the road. She'd probably open up when she felt more comfortable with him.

The next thing he knew, though, she had dropped her head into her hands, and the slim shoulders were heaving with sobs. He resisted the impulse to cover one of her small hands with his own.

"Want to tell me about it?" he shouted above the din in the cab. A torrent of rain poured from the overcast sky, driven by a gusty wind, and the wipers clacked noisily.

"I suppose I do owe you some kind of explanation," she mumbled, and Zach could barely make out her words. She lifted her head from her hands, and the blue eyes were enormous. "Let's just say that I was on the verge of making the biggest mistake of my life."

She sniffed, and Zach fumbled in his pocket, and dropped a big red bandana in her lap. She accepted it gratefully. After she blew her nose and wiped the tears from her face, she continued. "I finally found the courage to revolt when the minister started repeating the marriage vows. I realized I couldn't tie myself to someone I didn't love just to please my parents."

"No reason you should," Zach agreed.

"But what do I do now? The situation at home will be impossible."

"Do what you want to do. Aren't you 'free, white, and twenty-one,' as the old saying goes?" He halted at a stoplight. "Now, where is your house?"

She wiped steam off the window. "Right there. The one on the corner."

He pulled to a stop in front of a two-story brick dwelling

with a long walk edged in ivy. "Just a minute." He reached around behind the seat and, with a grin of triumph, produced a plastic poncho. "I wasn't an Eagle Scout for nothing!" he proclaimed. "Put this around your shoulders."

But when he opened her door, he gathered her into his arms and ran with her up the walkway to the awning-covered front door.

Having deposited her carefully, he stood close, shielding her shivering body with his own imposing frame. The pelting rain had found the vulnerable space between his thick brown hair and the collar of his jacket, so he hunched his shoulders, driving his hands into his pockets.

She looked down at her bedraggled finery and turned a brave but watery smile on him. "Well, sir, the service is superior. Have you ever considered starting your own company?"

Spunky little thing. She has a sense of humor. Unaccountably, his gaze was drawn to the wet clumps of dark lashes framing eyes that reminded him of the blue hyacinths growing down by the river in early spring. "As a matter of fact, I'm already in the transportation business."

He laughed, then shifted nervously from one foot to the other, his face sobering. "I don't suppose I'll ever see you again, but I'm going to pray that you'll be able to forget this day and start from scratch. There's no problem so big that you and God can't work it out together." He drew a long breath. "I don't blame you for running away from an impossible marriage, but on the other hand—" His voice grew husky, and he cleared his throat. "—I can't blame any man for wanting you, either." He stooped quickly and kissed her on the cheek, then turned on his heel and bolted down the walk.

Alisha watched him leave with an odd sense of loss. He vaulted into the truck, and pulled out into the street, lifting his hand in farewell. She tried to read the license plate, but she couldn't make it out through the downpour, though it looked like an out-of-state tag. She had already decided that her benefactor was not a native New Yorker, for his speech was flavored with an unusual dialect. He spoke slowly, with more mellow tones than she was used to, and he dropped his "g's," as if pronouncing the words precisely simply wasn't worth the trouble.

She watched his blue truck rumble off down the street. Too late, she realized that she hadn't asked his name, and that she was still clutching his red handkerchief in her hand.

With little time before her parents were likely to return from the church, Alisha shook off her speculations. She wouldn't waste time with thoughts of a man she would never see again. She rushed into the garage for the hidden key, let herself in, and ran upstairs to her room, unfastening the small pearl buttons on the way.

She surveyed the room, making hurried plans. Two packed suitcases stood by the door. Her going-away outfit waited in the closet. Slipping on the two-piece cotton knit dress, her conscience stirred. The ensemble was just the thing for a honeymoon flight, the saleslady had said, but this getaway was hardly the romantic scenario her mother had orchestrated.

Alisha telephoned for a taxi, then scribbled a note to her parents.

Dear Mother and Father,
   Please forgive me. I know I've disappointed you, but I couldn't go through with the wedding. Don't try to find me. I need some time to think things out.

Alisha

She propped the note on the dresser where it could be easily found, then searched her purse for the traveler's checks. The red bandana stood out vividly against the white bedspread, and she snatched it up and stuffed it into her purse.

The heavy suitcases bumped against her legs as she lugged them down the carpeted stairs. From the hallway wall, her sister stared at her with accusing eyes. Alisha looked away from the portrait. If she thought about Carol now, she'd never leave.

She fidgeted beside the front door for what seemed an interminable wait. Surely her parents would arrive home soon . . . or would the elaborate reception at the country club go on as planned? She felt another stab of guilt at the thought of the months of planning, not to mention the price tag on a society wedding.

By the time the taxi pulled into the driveway, the rain had slackened. With a sigh of relief, Alisha climbed in and settled back into the seat. No one would ever think to look for her at the bus terminal.

The pavement gleamed wet and shiny in the light mist. Alisha looked wistfully at the lawns aglow with blooming dogwood and flowering crab trees. Beds of tulips, still dripping from the deluge, raised their bright heads in defiance of the heavy shower. Buffalo was at its best in the spring, she thought with a growing sense of nostalgia.

Alisha lifted a shaking hand to wipe the tears from her eyes and bit her lip. In one reckless act, she might be closing the door forever on the only home she had ever known.

chapter

2

THE TOWN OF VANDALIA had given Alisha a quiet welcome the evening before, and in the dawning light of day, she looked with interest at the streets of the old city. There was no doubt of its age, for many of the buildings facing the River Hotel must have been built in the 1800s. The scarred red brick, the symmetrical façades, and the large squarish windows with many panes and dark shutters were reminiscent of a century ago.

From the second window of her corner room, she could see the river backing up to the hotel. Here, the Ohio River widened, and as she looked on, two boats met in mid-stream, whistles blaring. A smaller barge left the bank to come alongside the northern-bound vessel, and Alisha could see deck hands throwing ropes to crewmen on the larger craft. Several waterskiers zigzagged gracefully across the waves generated by the towboats. When one of the skiers tumbled into the water and disappeared from view, Alisha gasped and turned away.

She examined, instead, the steamboat pictures adorning the walls of her high-ceilinged room. From her studies, she knew that these were sternwheelers that came into usage after the Civil War. Interesting, she thought, that all of the boats bore the names of women—the *Kate Adams*, the Zelia Murphy, the *Anna Dee*.

As Alisha bathed and shampooed her hair, she reflected upon the intervening week since she had left Buffalo. The first night, in Pittsburgh, had been a harrowing experience. Unaccustomed to being alone, she had lifted the telephone once to call her parents, but summoning courage from some hidden source, had resisted the temptation to beg them to let her come home.

Keeping to herself, she had traveled aimlessly from one town to another, her final destination unknown until yesterday when she had overheard the conversation of two women in the bus station.

"I live in Vandalia, the most out-of-the-way place on earth," one of them had said to the other. "If you ever want to get away from the world, go to Vandalia."

That's the place for me, Alisha had decided, and she bought her ticket. Before the bus pulled out of the station, though, she was already doubting her decision. Where on earth was Vandalia? But when the bus arrived just at dusk, she was enchanted with the primitive charm of the small town.

One of the first things she had done after taking a room at the River Hotel was to assess her financial condition. It was obvious she would have to find work soon. With a degree in library science and no experience, her chances of finding a job seemed slim. Still, the hotel clerk had told her that the town had just opened a new library, and Alisha intended to follow up on the lead this very morning after breakfast.

She dressed hurriedly, but before she left her room to go down to the little coffee shop, she picked up the Bible lying on the nightstand and opened it to a now-familiar verse in the Book of Isaiah: "Say to those with fearful hearts, be strong, do not fear."

Remembering the words of the man who had come to her rescue on the tragic day of her wedding: "There's no problem so big that you and God can't work it out together," she had combed the Bible that first awful night in Pittsburgh until her eyes fell on that verse in the thirty-fifth chapter of Isaiah, and for the past few days, she had hugged those words to her. Strange, she thought, that though she had been a Christian since childhood, not until this experience had she realized she could call on God's power to order her daily life.

After breakfast, Alisha went upstairs to prepare for her interview. Intended for a Bermuda cruise, most of the clothes in her trousseau were too bare or too casual for business wear. She chose one of the more conservative ensembles that her mother had selected for afternoon occasions—a two-piece Liberty of Scotland print in blues and orchids. The shoulders of the bolero jacket were slightly padded, and the dirndl skirt flowed over her trim hips.

She looked in the mirror, tying and retying the bow of her pale lavender blouse at least three times before achieving the jaunty effect she was after. Then, tucking back an errant strand of hair, she surveyed her reflection with a critical eye. She knew that, despite her womanly curves, people often mistook her for a much younger woman. Satisfied that her outfit gave her the appearance of maturity, she slipped on a pair of high-heeled navy pumps and picked up a matching clutch purse.

But her confidence was short-lived. Reaching the door, she leaned weakly against it and murmured a desperate prayer: "Help me, Lord. You're the only One I have left." Then, lifting her head, she opened the door and stepped out into the hallway.

Outside, the day was warm with promise. Here, several hundred miles south of home, spring had a head start.

Dogwood trees planted along the uneven brick street had already dropped their petals, forming a pink carpet for several blocks.

As she walked along the sidewalk, Alisha perused the show windows of the shops lining the main street of town. At least two of the buildings housed antiques. There would be plenty of time to browse later. She fully intended to indulge her love of history in this fascinating place. But that would have to wait.

She picked up her pace and, following the instructions she had been given, had no trouble in locating the library. After stating her business to the bright-eyed young woman at the returns desk, she was asked to take a seat until the librarian could conclude an interview.

From her vantage point near the main desk where a small brass plaque spelled out "Nell Foster," Alisha could not help overhearing the conversation.

"I'm not long for this world," declared an elderly woman in a quavering voice. Eyes dulled with pain confirmed her self-prognosis. "Only the good Lord knows what my family will do with my belongin's. But these ... From a shabby handbag, she withdrew some papers that appeared to be as ancient and wrinkled as the woman herself. "I thought mebbe these might mean somethin' to some folks."

With great care, Nell Foster unfolded the documents. "Why, these are your great-grandfather's emancipation records!" she exclaimed.

"Yes'm. Thought you'd know how to keep 'em safe. An' before I pass, I'd like to tell the things I recollect from some of the old folks—like that underground tunnel where the slaves use' to hide. It's s'posed to be 'round these parts somewhere."

Alisha's pulse pounded. An underground tunnel! All her

instincts as an amateur historian and archeologist rose to the challenge. What she wouldn't give to find that old tunnel.

But Mrs. Foster was gently ushering the old woman to the front door, assuring her that she would protect her lifelong treasures. Alisha heard no more.

"Sorry you've had to wait." The librarian returned with a brisk step, her lively blue eyes alight with pleasure. "But that was a rare find, indeed. Besides, I'm really concerned about that old lady." A furrow in her brow was replaced by a wide smile. "Now, my dear, what can I do for you?"

"I guess the better question might be, 'What can *I* do for you?'" Alisha gave a wry smile. "I'm here to apply for a job . . . if there's anything available."

"Hmmm." Nell Foster tilted her head in an appraising manner. "Besides being very attractive, let's see what else you have to offer? Will you fill out this job application?"

With a sinking heart, Alisha filled out the brief form. When Mrs. Foster saw that Alisha's library science degree was less than a month old and that the sum total of her experience in the field consisted of a few semesters' internship in the university library, she was sure to be turned down flat.

Scanning the page, the librarian's next words had nothing to do with qualifications or credentials. "You're new in town, I see," she said conversationally, then turned an inquiring gaze on Alisha. "What brought you to Vandalia?"

For a long moment Alisha sat, gathering her thoughts. She wasn't ready to be confronted by her parents and their thousand and one questions and suggestions as to how she should spend the rest of her life. Still, the gray-haired lady with the twinkle in her eye seemed to invite trust.

Deciding on the honest approach, Alisha took a deep breath and held her voice steady. "I have some sorting out to do . . . on my own. This seemed the perfect place to do it."

"Quite right. Our town is as tranquil as they come these days, and the old cliché 'as quiet as a library' still applies." To Alisha's immense relief, the woman did not probe further, but turned again to the application form. "Now, suppose you tell me about your work at the university library."

"I assisted with historical research. The subject for my senior writing course was 'Finding and Cataloging the Past.'"

"Interesting." Alisha waited tensely while Mrs. Foster made a few notes on a yellow pad. "We may be able to use you," she said at last, and Alisha's heart lifted perceptibly, but the librarian's next words sent it plummeting again. "Unfortunately, we won't have an opening immediately. You see," she explained, "our town has been placed on the national roster of historic cities, and we plan to open a research section. We'll be collecting and cataloging documents to be used in our reading rooms. You're certainly well qualified for the work. . . . Right now we have boxes and boxes of such items stored in our attic. . . ." With mounting hope, Alisha watched Nell Foster twirling her pen absently. "However—" Again, there was that sinking sensation. "—we can't even begin to unpack them until September, when the federal funding for our program becomes available."

"September!" Alisha gasped. "That's three months away!"

"I know, my dear, and I'm as disappointed as you are. I think you could be a real asset. Why not check back with us at the end of the summer?" She rose in dismissal.

Alisha felt her tenuous composure slipping. Her head throbbed, and there was a knot in the pit of her stomach. Nevertheless, she stood and extended her hand. "Well, thank you, Mrs. Foster. You've been very kind. But I'd like to ask one thing more if I may."

"Of course."

"Could you possibly suggest where I might find some kind of work in the meantime?"

"I'd really like to help you. . . ." Nell Foster posed, one hand pressed to her temple in contemplation. At last she brightened. "It just might work," she said, as if responding to some kind of inner prompting. "There may still be a position on the showboat."

"Showboat?"

"Yes. As a part of a special state celebration this summer, a showboat will travel the waterways, presenting dramatic scenes from our historical heritage, along with music and entertainment. With your background, you should be a natural."

"But I don't have any experience as an actress."

Nell Foster shrugged. "I don't have the particulars. You'd have to see Paul Blair, the co-owner of the boat. I think he does the hiring. Why not give it a try? The boat is docked right behind the River Hotel."

Alisha willed a smile and found that only the corners of her mouth obeyed. "Thank you again. I'll be in touch about the possibility of a job this fall. Now—" She squared her shoulders, speaking more to herself than to the kindly woman behind the desk. "—to find out what kind of stuff I'm really made of."

The showboat was a beehive of activity, and Alisha hesitated at the gangplank that would give her access to the handsome vessel. From bow to stern, the craft gleamed a glistening white that exaggerated its size. Two decks carried the eye upward to the small pilot house poised on top. The name, *The Mountain Laurel*, splashed boldly across the side in blue letters. Near the water level, walkways ran the length and breadth of the boat and continued along the upper deck.

Paradoxically, the effect was both sturdy strength and slender grace.

Alisha took a tentative step onto the gangplank but reversed her direction hastily when the narrow board swayed beneath her weight. Beads of perspiration popped out on her forehead. *What are you waiting for?* she scolded. *For some gallant knight to carry you across like that workman with his load of wood?*

She stepped aside to admit a carpenter carrying two wooden panels on his shoulder and holding a saw in one hand. Whistling, he crossed the bouncing platform without slowing his gait.

Small chance, my girl. It's up to you. Everybody's busy with his own life. Now, are you going to walk across that gangplank, or are you going to be a coward for the rest of your life?

With eyes focused straight ahead, not daring to glance at the small swells lapping at the hull, she crossed to the deck of the boat.

Releasing the breath she had been holding, she looked around to get her bearings. To one side was another workman applying a coat of gray paint to a section of deck. Upon closer inspection, Alisha saw that the figure garbed in loose-fitting coveralls was feminine. Beneath the man's cap she wore, one long strand of red hair had escaped and floated over her shoulder.

"Hi!" she called when she spotted Alisha. "You can walk across that end. I haven't painted that part yet."

"Thanks." Alisha nodded, noting the dusting of freckles across a pert nose. "I'm looking for Paul Blair."

"That's my dad. I'm Tammy Blair. He's at the top of those steps. You'll find him in the office . . . first door on the left."

Alisha found the place easily enough and, seeing that the man was preoccupied with a sheaf of papers on his desk, dropped into the chair he indicated with a brusque gesture. While he completed his reading, she had time to look about the room.

Navigation charts and boxes of papers cluttered the space, which was small but efficiently arranged. Still, Alisha thought the high-tech computer and printer contrasted oddly with the heavy old oak furniture, etched with a scroll-type design and burnished to a golden sheen from years of use.

"If only they'd cut some of the confounded red tape, we might be able to get this show on the road, but when you fool with the federal government, there's always busywork!" he grumbled under his breath.

She turned her attention to the man at the desk. Paul Blair's red hair was thinning at the forehead; his ruddy face was beardless and covered with freckles.

"Well, that's done," he said, as he shoved the papers aside. "And now what can I do for you, young lady?"

"I'm looking for summer employment, and I heard you might be needing some additional staff . . . crew?" She fumbled for the proper term.

He grinned. "Know anything about riverboats?"

"No, sir. This is the first time I've ever been on one."

"Know anything about acting?"

"No, sir."

"Know anything about cooking, swabbing down a deck, directing a show?"

"No." Her voice was as low as her spirits. This was useless.

"You don't know much of anything, do you?"

His words stung her into action. "Obviously, I don't," she said as she stood up and started for the door. "Sorry I bothered you."

"Sit down," he said and, seeing that his blue eyes sparkled, she paused. "You're the kind of person I'm looking for.

Know-it-alls don't get very far on the *Laurel*. Do you have any idea of our plans for the summer?"

Alisha felt herself relaxing. "Not really," she admitted. "The only clue I have is what the librarian told me. I applied for work at the library, but was told they couldn't use me until September at the very earliest. Mrs. Foster suggested I might find something here. In the meantime—" She spread her hands wide. "—I have to eat. I'm curious, too. What, exactly, *will* you be doing on this boat?"

"Putting on performances." He got right to the point. "Isn't that the purpose of a showboat?"

"I suppose so. I know river theatricals were popular after the Civil War. But, frankly, I thought they were a thing of the past."

"I see you know your history, at least," Paul said approvingly. "My family entered the business much later that that, though. The Blairs and the Martins built the *Laurel* around the turn of the century. She's traveled the Ohio, the Mississippi, and a dozen other rivers. After World War II, the showboat craze ended, and this craft became obsolete. For nostalgic reasons, more than anything else, we kept the old girl tied up at some property we own along the Ohio, about fifteen miles north of Vandalia. In fact, my mother lived aboard the boat."

Alisha registered her surprise with a lifted brow. "Pretty big house for one person, isn't it?"

"She used only a few rooms, but even at that we couldn't prevent deterioration. At least we kept the old relic afloat. Then, when our state decided to observe this year as a 'Salute to Transportation,' officials asked us to bring out the *Laurel* to focus on the importance of river travel in the development of our area. Sounded good to us . . . and to the Martins." He rose and paced the narrow room. "We decided that, if we could obtain federal funds for renovation at the end of the season, we'd donate the boat to the town of Vandalia for a museum. The civic leaders plan to use part of it for a restaurant. Should be a pretty profitable tourist attraction."

He paused, and Alisha realized he had come to the end of his monologue. "It certainly sounds like a good idea," she said. "But I think I've come to the wrong place. I doubt that I could make much of a contribution."

"Hold on." He held up a hand, and his voice took on a stern note. "You need to know, up front, that the pay is peanuts. You'd get room and board, of course, but no crew member gets rich, and you'd be expected to work hard, both in rehearsal and at odd jobs when you're not performing. With our limited staff, everyone pitches in with the chores."

"But that's just the problem. Oh, I don't mean the chores. I'm no pampered socialite." She thought fleetingly of the honeymoon cruise she would have been experiencing at this very moment, with an entire staff at her beck and call. And Theodore, too. She hurried on. "I really want to work for you, but I'm afraid I'm not a performer."

He swung into his swivel chair and spun to face her, his blue eyes boring into her. "Can you sing? Play a musical instrument?"

"Well . . . I played the trumpet in our high school band. With some practice, I might remember how. And I sang in the college choir." Her voice rose with growing conviction.

The idea of spending the summer aboard this boat was becoming more attractive by the moment. What better place to hide from the world than behind grease paint, assuming the identity of some character from another era? Besides, she would have a place to stay until the library job materialized.

"Then, I'm satisfied if you are. Nell Foster's recommendation is good enough for me." The boyish grin was disarming.

"Can you move your gear aboard by tonight? We start rehearsals in the morning." At her eager nod, the smile left his lips. "By the way—" *What is it this time?* she wondered uneasily as her emotions took another nosedive. *Does the man need help or not?* "You'd have to bunk with another gal. No doubt she had a dollop of gray paint on her nose if you ran into her below. My daughter, Tammy. This cruise is her high school graduation present."

"Oh," she sighed in relief, "is that all? I've already met her, and she's adorable. I wouldn't mind at all."

At that moment an unearthly shriek shattered the stillness of the tiny room.

"What on earth is *that?*"

Paul spoke above the noise. "That's our calliope player. He's a little rusty as you can tell." He laughed at her contorted face. "You'll get used to it."

Still laughing, Paul went on. "The calliope is the symbol of showboat travel; we couldn't do without it. There," he said with satisfaction, as the music settled into a faintly recognizable melody. "I believe he's got the hang of it now."

Alisha grimaced. "Still sounds like something that needs oiling to me. I'll bring my things from the hotel and be back soon. Thanks again, Mr. Blair, for giving me this opportunity. I'll try not to disappoint you." *If you can pull that off, Alisha DeFoe, it'll be the first time,* she thought, realizing with fresh grief that she had brought nothing but disappointment to her parents.

As she started down the steps, Alisha spotted a large group of children gathered on the bank listening to the music as it reverberated across the water. She supposed the showboat was quite a wonder to them. The calliope was sounding better all the time.

Tammy had almost finished her painting and laid a board

31

across the wet paint for Alisha. "Hi, again! Did Dad hire you?"

"Not only that, but I think you're stuck with me for a roommate."

"Great!" Tammy seemed genuinely pleased. "Maybe Dad will let us do a duet or something." She struck an operatic pose. "You moving in tonight?"

"Just as soon as I can get my luggage from the hotel."

"Super! We start working on the show tomorrow."

Alisha crossed the gangplank with only slightly less apprehension than she had experienced earlier, but she still kept her gaze averted from the river. Perhaps she'd be forced to get over her fear of water if she worked on a boat all summer.

As she started up the bank to the hotel, the tune from the calliope changed abruptly. Strident strains of "My Old Kentucky Home" shifted to the hauntingly familiar melody of Lohengrin's "Wedding March." Alisha halted in her tracks.

Powerless to resist the impulse to look back, she turned to see if she could catch a glimpse of the calliope player. The tall figure standing before a series of copper pipes lifted his hand and brought it to his forehead in a snappy salute. Even from this distance she could see his lips parting in a bright smile, framed by a neatly clipped beard.

"Oh, no," Alisha moaned, her heart flutterkicking before sinking completely. *The truck driver who helped me when I ran away from the wedding!*

Though she scarcely knew the man, he was a part of the past she was trying so desperately to forget. If she reported to work, she would be reminded of that tragic day for the rest of the summer. Reaching the top of the incline, she broke into a run.

"Hey!" A masculine voice from behind drove her faster— past the hotel, down the tree-lined street. Hearing his sprinting footsteps hard on her heels, she gasped as a strong hand grasped her arm and spun her about. "Running again? You're sure one determined lady. I've never seen anyone so bent on getting somewhere in a big hurry!"

She looked up into the chocolate brown eyes, tiny lines radiating from the corners.

"Of all the places on earth, why did I have to pick the one place I'd run into you?" she sputtered indignantly.

"I've got a hunch it's because I've been praying that the Lord would arrange some way for us to meet again. But I must admit he usually doesn't work this fast!" He chuckled, and in spite of her protest, the resonant voice flowed like warm honey over her bruised spirit.

"Well, I don't think it's all that funny," Alisha said crossly. "I needed that job with Mr. Blair's showboat. Now, I won't be able to take it. This summer, I didn't want to see anyone who knows me." She was very near tears.

Instantly, he produced a look of dismay, took a step backward, and covered his heart with his hand. "Who, me? Why, ma'am, I don't know you. I don't even know your name."

At this display of theatrics, Alisha relaxed a little.

"Furthermore, there's no reason you can't work wherever you want," he added.

She gave him a searching look. "If I stay . . . will you promise not to tell anybody what you know about me?"

"Scout's honor!" he said and lifted his hand in a three-fingered pledge. "You ought to know by now, I don't take advantage of strange women."

Alisha couldn't stifle the giggle that erupted from her throat. "So now I'm strange!" The sound was foreign to her own ears. How long had it been since she had found anything even remotely amusing?

"Maybe now's as good a time as any for introductions. I'm Zach Martin."

"Martin? As in Blair and Martin . . . of riverboat fame?"

"The same, at your service." He bowed formally. "Except this summer, I'll be known as the guy who pilots the towboat for the *Laurel*, and tinkers around with the calliope, of course." He grinned.

Alisha could feel the beginnings of a warm glow. She extended her hand daintily and made a mock curtsey. "And I'm Alisha DeFoe, newest member of the troupe."

"Welcome to Vandalia, Alisha." He placed his lips lightly on her hand, and she could feel the soft caress of his mustache. Straightening, he said briskly, "Now, let's get your things and hightail it back to the boat. Your public is waiting."

chapter
3

THE ROOM ALISHA SHARED WITH Tammy was little more than a cubbyhole. A set of bunk beds lined one side of the room, while a dresser, two chairs, and a built-in closet completed the Spartan arrangement.

"No bathroom?" Alisha inquired.

"Sure. Down the hall." Tammy gestured with a cocked thumb.

Well, at least my roommate is an improvement over Theodore Blevins, Alisha thought with determined good humor. Noting the cramped space, she said, "I suppose I shouldn't have brought both of these cases."

"No problem. Unpack what you think you'll need, and we'll stow the rest in one of the vacant rooms. You probably won't need much except jeans and shirts most of the time. When we're in the show, we'll be in costume."

Alisha lifted a few items from the first case. She certainly hadn't packed any work clothes. Her mother had suggested only the most elegant cruisewear, designed for romantic evenings and sun-spangled days, and, Alisha suspected, with an eye toward impressing Theodore.

Tammy had been reclining on the bottom bunk, and she moved over to the closet and shoved her clothing to one side.

"On second thought," she amended, "maybe you'd better hang up as much as you can. Sometimes we get to go ashore to see the sights. You'll need some changes then." Stripping sheets from the bottom bunk, Tammy continued, "I've been sleeping down below, but I don't mind bunking on top. Ever sleep on a boat before?"

"No," Alisha answered, thinking with some amusement of the contrast with the luxurious honeymoon cruise planned for this week.

"Did you come to West Virginia to work on the boat, or what?" Tammy asked without a hint of snoopiness. "You aren't a native, that's for sure. You talk funny."

"Do I?" She smiled at the impish young woman whose own brogue was equally "funny" in Alisha's mind. "Actually," she went on in answer to Tammy's question, "I'd never heard of the *Laurel* until yesterday. After college, it just seemed a change was in order," she explained, carefully omitting any mention of the aborted wedding. "So I struck out with no particular destination in mind and . . . fell in love with Vandalia at first sight."

"Good choice, too." Tammy tucked in the sheets on the upper bunk and plopped down, cross-legged, on the bed.

Alisha took off the dress she'd worn all day and changed into designer jeans and a blue knit shirt.

"You sure have some classy clothes," Tammy said just as a gong sounded. She jumped to the floor. "Good grief! It's suppertime already, and I forgot to help Ma . . . that's my grandmother. I'll catch the dickens for that if she tells Dad. Let's go. You don't dare be late for meals around here."

Tammy couldn't have been more than three or four years younger than Alisha, but beside the young woman's bustling vitality, Alisha felt light-years older. With difficulty, she followed as the pert redhead bounded down a flight of steps to the lower deck, then led the way along a narrow walkway right on the water's edge. Alisha cringed but tried to forget the river under her feet. A narrow bridge gave them access to the smaller towboat, and Alisha trailed behind, holding tenaciously to the flimsy handrail.

"I don't know what your duties will be around here, but could you lend me a hand?" Tammy asked. "Ma will be needing help putting food on the table for this mob."

Alisha entered the snow-white galley where an older woman with a flowered apron tied around her ample girth was spooning mashed potatoes into large bowls. The aroma of fried chicken reminded Alisha that it had been a long time since breakfast.

"Sorry I'm late, Ma," Tammy said. "This is Alisha DeFoe. Dad just hired her today. And this is my grandmother, Sarah Blair. She'll be our cook this summer, but don't let that fool you. She runs this boat, and everybody on it, including my Dad . . . though he'd never admit it!" She grinned affectionately at the woman, grabbed two bowls of potatoes, and headed into the dining area.

"Nice to meet you, dear," Ma said. "Now, the two of you hustle this grub out to those hungry sailors."

In addition to the potatoes, the fare consisted of heaping platters of fried chicken, green beans, creamed corn, cole slaw, biscuits, plenty of iced tea and coffee, and thick servings of apple pie. By the time the tables had been served, at least twenty people had filed into the room and stood at their places until Paul Blair's arrival.

"Zach, how about saying the blessing?"

At Paul's suggestion, the hum of voices hushed, and Zach's voice rang out, confident and clear.

Busy as she had been, Alisha hadn't noticed his entrance into the room, but she listened now with something akin to awe. She had never known anyone who appeared to be on such intimate terms with God. Evidently, Zach Martin spent a lot of time talking to his heavenly Father.

Between bites, Alisha stayed busy replenishing the serving bowls and filling glasses with the cold beverages. There was little opportunity to chat or get acquainted with her fellow travelers. Once, she passed Zach's table, and he flashed her a bright smile. "They're breaking you in, I see."

The meal ended with an announcement from Paul Blair. "We'll meet in the theater in forty-five minutes."

There was a mass exodus shortly thereafter, and Alisha lost sight of Zach for the moment. She helped with the stacking of plates, carrying them to the serving counter near the galley, where two young men swished water over the dirty dishes and inserted them into a restaurant-sized dishwasher.

"Let's sit on the roof until time for the meeting." Tammy led the way to the top deck where some canvas folding chairs had been placed near the pilot house.

"You don't have to spend all your time with me," Alisha insisted. "I'm sure you must have other friends you'd like to visit."

Tammy stretched out on one of the canvas chairs. "Not really. I don't know many more of these people than you do. Most of them are from the drama department at the university, and they've only been here since yesterday."

"Then the students will be doing all the acting in the shows?" Alisha asked hopefully.

"Oh, we'll have to do some acting, too. Didn't Dad tell you that you'd be expected to do a little bit of everything?" Tammy looked around the boat as if memorizing every detail. "This summer is a dream come true for me. All my life I've heard about the great showboating days of the Blairs and the

Martins, but I didn't suppose I'd ever get a chance to find out what it was like, firsthand."

"Your dad mentioned that his family and the Martins had been partners."

"They still are." She placed her hands behind her head and looked up into the twilit sky. "The Martins and the Blairs have been friends for generations. In fact, my older sister married Zach's brother. The families own a fleet of diesels, but Dad took a leave of absence from his regular job to run this boat. He usually works on the *Roberta Blair,* named for my mother. We'll see it a lot this summer, between Cincinnati and Pittsburgh." Cocking an inquisitive eye toward Alisha, she ventured a question. "Say, have you ever met Zach before?"

Alisha blushed. "Only once . . . but I didn't know his name or where he lived."

"Well, I thought you might have come here because . . . well, you know . . . because you had a crush on him, and I was going to tell you to forget—"

The sound of approaching footsteps interrupted Tammy's speech, and Alisha welcomed the diversion. Zach's head popped into view, and Alisha felt a rush of pleasure. Why did she feel she had known this man forever?

"Good grief!" Tammy cried. "Are you going to play that thing?" She motioned toward the arrangement of copper pipes at the stern of the boat. "We came up here to rest, but little rest we'll get with that racket you call music!"

Zach thumped Tammy on the head with his finger. "I came to lock the pilot house for the night, brat." He turned to Alisha. "Want to see the calliope? It's one of the very few left on the rivers. Some in museums, but they're a thing of the past," he said with obvious regret.

Alisha nodded. "I'd like that. I haven't seen one before."

Zach led the way toward the rear of the boat. "The instrument consists of a series of graduated whistles with valves pitched to produce the various notes of the scale," he explained, pointing out the features. "Steam actually provides the sound, so we have a special little boiler just for the calliope."

"But how does it work?" Alisha asked. The instrument was by far the strangest looking she had ever seen.

"The valves are inserted at intervals in the top of this V-shaped feed valve. See? Right here. They're connected to the keyboard." He indicated a bank of keys more than two feet wide. "When I press a certain key, the valve connected to it releases steam into the appropriate whistle to produce the desired note. It's been so long since I've played the thing that I've forgotten a lot, but I'll get the knack of it in a few more days . . . if the rest of you can stand it that long." He patted the instrument fondly. "Sometimes I'll play as we cruise . . . to let people know well in advance that the showboat is coming."

"Time to go," Tammy said as she headed for the stairs. "You know how grumpy Dad is if anyone's late." She darted on ahead.

Dusk blanketed the boat, and river sounds lent their own special music to the tranquil scene. Frogs grumbled in the shallow water along the bank, and a cardinal, perched on a tree limb overhanging the river, began a farewell song to the day. The clear notes penetrated the hard core around Alisha's heart, and she felt the sting of tears. She hesitated when Zach started down the steps.

"Something wrong, honey?" He looked around, a frown of concern furrowing his brow.

"I guess I'm a little nervous. This is all so new, and with all that's happened—"

"Hey, take it easy. I'll be around if you need any help. Aren't we buddies?" He gave her a conspiratorial wink. "And isn't it time you stopped running? Just relax, honey. Everything's going to be all right."

"I hope so, Zach. Oh, I hope so!" She hugged her arms about herself against the sudden night chill.

chapter
4

THE WALLS OF THE THEATER were painted in blue and gold, a theme repeated in the striped upholstery covering the opera chairs. Plush blue carpet padded the aisles, and concealed lights provided a dim glow as Alisha groped uncertainly down the corridor, toward the group gathering near a stage draped with heavy maroon curtains.

"This theater holds three hundred people," Zach said, "and we could seat another fifty in the balcony. In the old days, the poorer patrons sat there, but that's where we keep the spotlights now."

Paul introduced the assembled cast and crew, but Alisha had trouble putting names with faces. She did take note of Mike and Jane Price, however.

"Mike is the drama coach at the university, where he directs their public presentations and also acts in the plays," Paul explained. "Jane is an actress, as well as chairperson of the university's music department."

The Prices appeared to be in their mid-thirties. Jane was slender and tall, towering several inches over her husband, a wiry man whose lean frame suggested that he spent a lot of time jogging.

When Paul had finished the introductions, his countenance

42

darkened slightly. "In case there is any confusion about who's in charge, I'm the boss." A laugh softened the declaration. "At those times when I'm not aboard, I'm appointing Mike and Zach as second in command. Mike, as director, makes all decisions about programming. Anything connected with the operation of the boat is Zach's concern, and I suppose that Ma will boss all of us most of the time. After all, we've taken over her home for the summer."

Alisha felt the gentle sway of the boat beneath them, and she supposed that the rocking movement had been caused by a passing towboat. After the stressful day, she thought longingly of the bunk that was to be her bed for the next few weeks.

"One more thing—" Paul warned, "—everybody works on this boat. There are no 'stars.' At least two people will be responsible for each part, whether major or minor. In addition to performing, all of you will be expected to do your share of routine chores. Check the work schedule, and don't fail to report to your post promptly."

Paul went on to detail the on-board duties. Four of the young men would work with Zach on the towboat. Tammy and Alisha, under Ma's supervision, were responsible for buying the groceries and for serving the food.

Rehearsals would begin in the morning and continue for the next five days while they were docked at Vandalia. Once the showboat was underway, two hours each day would be devoted to practice.

"We'll open here in Vandalia, then cruise south as far as Cincinnati, taking two days for travel from one city to the next. On our return, we'll stop over at Pittsburgh. If all goes as planned, our final performance will be staged back here on Labor Day. Bon voyage. Now, let's get some sleep!"

In the flurry of activity during the following week, Alisha had little time for anything except the task at hand. There were groceries and other supplies to buy and stash away in the efficiently designed galley, menus to plan, and, of course, rehearsals for the production itself.

"The show we've chosen was written especially for presentation by a showboat troupe," Paul explained the next morning. "The tourist bureau and I spent a considerable amount of time selecting just the right one." Pausing dramatically, he waited until he had the full attention of the cast before continuing. "I know rumors have been flying about the production. Let me lay them all to rest. The title is 'Where Rivers Flow.'" A buzz of excited chatter followed the announcement. "You'll find that this drama differs from the old-time vaudeville shows that were so popular at the turn of the century, with several actors performing individual acts. Eventually, the actors presented melodramas such as 'Uncle Tom's Cabin' and 'Ten Nights in a Barroom.'"

"And don't forget that a few even tried some Shakespeare," Ma interjected.

The older woman would perform in a few scenes, but her acting wouldn't interfere with her cooking, Alisha was relieved to hear. The food was simple, but delicious. Glancing at her now, Alisha saw that she sat with a pan of potatoes in her lap, busily peeling the vegetables as she waited for her cue.

"Well, we may even resort to Shakespeare ourselves if this show doesn't appeal to the audiences, but I think our audiences will like our focus on river transportation. We'll throw in some vaudeville and a little melodrama, too."

"What about local history?" Mike asked, leaning forward.

Paul nodded in acknowledgment. "At Parkersburg, we'll add a scene dealing with the history of Blennerhassett Island."

"Blennerhassett Island?" Alisha whispered to Tammy. "Never heard of it."

"That's because you're not a West Virginian. It's an island in the Ohio River . . . connected with Aaron Burr. You've heard of him, haven't you?"

"Will you two girls pay attention?" Paul scolded with mock severity.

Tammy gave Alisha a furtive wink as she turned her attention to her father.

"And we'll include a scene featuring the character of Stephen Foster at Pittsburgh, his birthplace." Paul wiped his brow with a handkerchief, as if the enormity of the task were already pressing heavily. "Basically, we'll give the same show each evening, but we'll vary the performances occasionally, especially at large cities where we'll spend two nights. And, in addition to the scenes of local historical interest, the drama department is working on the most famous of all the old melodramas, 'Ten Nights in a Barroom.' We'll be doing that one later on in the summer."

"Wow!" Alisha dared Paul's displeasure and whispered to Tammy, "I can see now why we have to practice every day."

Later on, Alisha fidgeted behind the scenes while the university students auditioned and received their roles. They would have the major parts and earn six credit hours for the summer's work.

Despite Paul's insistence that everyone was needed on stage, Alisha figured he'd change his mind when he observed her acting ability. But after listening to Alisha sing a couple of songs and trying her voice with Tammy, who sang a pleasing alto, Mike said, "You'll be fine in some of the singing acts." And he set her to practicing several numbers with Zach, who seemed to be a regular one-man band.

He was seated at the upright piano now, running through

some old show tunes with a practiced touch. He winked as she approached, her insecurity showing.

"This won't hurt a bit," he promised, handing her a piece of sheet music. "Let's try this one."

"Well, don't say I didn't warn you." Alisha cleared her throat nervously and sang the melody line, gaining volume as her confidence grew.

"Hey, hold down that note, honey," he suggested at one point. "That's supposed to be a softie. Want to drive the audience out of their seats?"

She took no offense at first, but was grateful for his direction. And when he was equally quick with praise, she felt herself flushing with pleasure.

Once, when he criticized her interpretation of a particularly difficult passage, she couldn't hold back the tears.

Instantly, he was on his feet and at her side, a protective arm about her shoulders. "Why, honey. I didn't mean to bawl you out. . . . Just want to make you a great star."

"I don't want to be a great star," Alisha sniffled. "I don't think I can get up on that stage and sing in front of an audience, anyway. I'd better stick to the kitchen work and leave the performing to someone else." She laid the music down on top of the piano.

But he picked it up and forced it back into her hands. "Don't do it, Alisha. Don't run away again."

On Sunday morning, all activity on the *Laurel* ceased, and at breakfast, Paul invited the cast to a worship service in the dining area. "It's not compulsory, you understand, but everyone is welcome."

With some misgivings, Alisha showed up with a handful of others and was surprised to see Zach at the front of the room, guitar in hand. Without preamble, he closed his eyes and strummed the strings, humming an old gospel hymn. In the stillness of the room, he began to sing:

> Holy Spirit, breathe on me,
> Until my heart is clean;
> Let sunshine fill its inmost part,
> With not a cloud between.
> Breathe on me, breathe on me,
> Holy Spirit, breathe on me;
> Take thou my heart, cleanse ev'ry part,
> Holy Spirit, breathe on me.

When Zach moved into a familiar number, they joined him on the chorus, but Alisha sat mute, listening to the clear sweet tenor soaring above the others.

At the finish of the song, Zach laid down the guitar and picked up a Bible. Flipping through the pages, he paused at one passage and began to read: " 'If the Son sets you free, you will be free indeed.' That's from John's gospel, the eighth chapter. In the book of Galatians," he said, turning over a few more pages, "Paul says this: 'It is for freedom that Christ has set us free. Stand firm, then, and do not let yourselves be burdened again by a yoke of slavery.' "

Zach quickly sketched the background of the book of Galatians, explaining how the Christians of that time had relied on their good works to save them, wanting to live the Christian life but bound by certain Old Testament ceremonies.

Alisha had been drinking in the message, captivated as much by the truth he was revealing as by the heart-stopping speaker himself. But it was Zach's next words that broke her heart.

"What are the things that make people slaves today?" he asked. "What about our weaknesses, our guilt, our lack of faith, our fears?" Burning with zeal, his brown eyes roamed the room. His gaze fell on Alisha, and she felt the intensity of his compassion. "If Christ is Lord of your life, you have nothing to fear, you know," he said quietly, as if speaking to Alisha alone. "And the guilt that plagues you can be blown away by the freedom you have in him. He wants to set us free to love and serve him . . . and each other." He paused, and the room was utterly still. "As we sing, try to let go of anything that has enslaved you . . . anything that stands as a barrier between you and your Lord."

Alisha could feel the sting of hot tears. She opened her mouth to join in the closing chorus, but she couldn't utter a sound. And, as the soft melody flowed over the group, she received the cleansing tide of God's Spirit. For the first time she felt light and free . . . free from her mother's cloying domination, free from her own long-held guilt over her sister's death.

After a short prayer, Alisha kept her head bowed, the tears tracing a wet path down her face. At the touch of Zach's hand on her arm, she looked up.

"Anything I can do to help?"

"You already have. I'm remembering what you told me in—" She paused to look around, but no one else was listening. "—in Buffalo. 'There isn't anything so difficult that God and I can't work it out together.' Well, he must have led me here to this boat, if for no other reason than to hear what you had to say this morning."

The deep peace radiating from her sweet face, the shining eyes, the dark hair haloed by a stream of sunbeams through the window broke the wall of resistance Zach had been trying hard to maintain. His outward reserve was nothing but a façade, he knew. His heart started a triphammer pace. *There is no place in your life for this woman,* he cautioned himself. *Don't let her get to you.*

Alisha knew she would be singing in the chorus, but her acting roles came as a surprise—a non-speaking part in a Shawnee village scene, a few lines in a scene featuring the flatboat era, and a short speech in a scene depicting the antebellum South. Tammy would be playing in the same scenes, and since all the parts required some study, she and her roommate spent their evenings with scripts propped up in front of them, lounging on their bunks and reciting lines.

"Tomorrow we'll pick out our costumes," Tammy said one night. "There's a little dressing room backstage. We'll store the outfits there, as well as dress for the shows."

"Are the costumes very expensive?" Alisha asked, thinking of her dwindling supply of money.

"Not to worry." Tammy climbed down from the top bunk and poured herself a glass of Coke. "The federal grant covers everything. All we have to do is choose what we want from the costume rental agency in town."

The Indian costume wasn't much more than a burlap bag, Alisha decided when they made their foray into Vandalia the next day, but she spotted a hoop-skirted gown of pale blue satin for her southern belle role that would more than compensate. By the time they were ready to leave the rental agency, she had an armload of costumes—the burlap, the satin, two calico dresses with matching bonnets from the frontier era, and a stunning outfit worn by actresses in the gay 90s. She felt her heart lift with an unexpected thrill of anticipation, imagining herself in the various roles she would be playing.

Despite this small burst of enthusiasm, Alisha still felt

somewhat of an outsider during the following week. Except for Paul, Zach, and Tammy, she didn't really know any of her fellow crew members. That wasn't all bad, she decided. With no time for exchanging confidences, there were no questions about her past to answer. And in the hectic pace of her routine, it was easy to submerge all her energies in the present and forget the unhappiness she had left in her wake at home.

Not that the people from the university intentionally excluded her, but every evening they gravitated toward each other in a makeshift classroom to discuss the day's performance. To receive college credit for the tour, students had to attend a daily seminar. And when they were thrown together with the others during performances, they existed in a make-believe world, more often than not calling each other by their stage names rather than their real ones.

She thought of Ma, who treated her with the same fond regard she held for her own granddaughter, and of Tammy, who had accepted her as a surrogate sister almost from the day they had met. Once, when she had commented on this strange phenomenon to Zach, he had said, "You're in Appalachia now, honey. Folks are friendly down *here*.

Alisha's nerves were frazzled the night of dress rehearsal, but the performance went to Paul's satisfaction. Several of the drama students even complimented Alisha on her presentations. While she gratefully accepted their plaudits, she knew that acting was not her forté.

At the close of the last scene, she glanced about distractedly for the one person whose opinion mattered most. Zach was nowhere in sight.

"Hi there, Sarah Bernhardt," he said, slipping up behind her. "Since this is our last free evening, I thought we could go ashore for a while. We'll get plenty tired of this scow before the summer is over."

"Sounds interesting." She was glad for the dim lighting. She had felt a rush of heat to her cheeks at his greeting. "Just give me time to change."

"Twenty minutes enough?" At her nod, he added, "Meet you at the gangplank."

In the small dressing room, she raced through her costume change.

"Hmmm. Must be a heavy date," Tammy observed. "What's the hurry?"

"Zach asked me to go to town with him," Alisha answered nonchalantly, applying a generous dollop of cleansing cream to remove the heavy make-up. "Your dad won't mind if we leave the boat, will he?"

Tammy shrugged. "Why should he? He loves to play the dictator, but he really isn't." Alisha envied their easy camaraderie. Tammy and her father bickered a lot, but there was little doubt of the close bond between them. Tammy often mentioned her mother, Roberta, too, but it was clear that there was a special relationship between father and daughter.

Alisha hurried upstairs to the stateroom, changing into pale yellow slacks and a matching blouse. Having discovered that the summer breezes were often chilly, she shrugged on a sweater. Inspecting her reflection in the mirror, she saw that her casual hairstyle needed little more than a quick brushing. Fortunately, humid air only enhanced its natural curl.

"Why the fuss?" she asked her reflection. "This is not much of a date."

But she couldn't conceal the sudden surge of pleasure at the thought of the handsome bearded man waiting for her below.

She found him near the gangplank, and he took her arm as if he sensed her terror. She would never get used to that swaying piece of timber suspended over the water, it seemed.

Safely on shore, Zach loosed his grasp on her elbow. "Let's

just walk, shall we? Not much to do in Vandalia, but I thought we could stop for a Coke later."

They strolled quietly, content to listen to the sighing sounds of the breeze riffling the leaves and a chorus of crickets nearby. Few lights punctuated the night, and at times they walked in total darkness. Zach's nearness dispelled any fear Alisha might have known.

As they came in sight of one of the century-old houses, illuminated by carriage lights mounted on either side of the arched doorway, Alisha spoke. "I wonder how old this town is."

"I'm not sure of the date, but the town was incorporated before the Civil War. Many of the houses along this street were built in the 1800s. Vandalia was in its heyday during the steamboat era, but people have lived in this area since the first settlers came across the Appalachian mountains."

"Have your people been here that long?"

He took Alisha's arm to steady her across a rough spot in the street, and his touch triggered a tremor of excitement. "We've been around a long time. One of my ancestors settled in the valley during the Revolutionary War, and my father's people arrived a few years before the War Between the States."

In the flicker of a random streetlight, they paused to read the sign on an old brick building. "'Once the site of a station for the Underground Railroad,'" Alisha read aloud, and her eyes glowed with interest. "Buffalo was one of the northern-most points for the Railroad; I did a research paper on that in college. But I never expected to see one of the stations at the other end of the line."

Alisha remembered the words of the black woman who had mentioned an underground tunnel to Nell Foster, the librarian. Just as she opened her mouth to ask Zach what he might know about it, he launched into another discussion. "The Ohio River served as a boundary line between slave and free states. If the slaves made it across the river, they could enjoy some degree of freedom."

"I guess this state would have been slave territory. Did your family ever own slaves?"

"Hardly," Zach replied with a laugh. "They were abolition-ists—not too popular in this area before the Civil War."

They made a short circle and entered the business district again, where Zach paused at a small restaurant. "Want to take a break?"

As they seated themselves at a booth in the back of the café, Alisha remarked, "I was thinking how unusual to be able to wander around the streets without worrying about being mugged. In Buffalo, that's a problem everywhere."

"One of the advantages of a small town, honey." He lifted a dark brow. "Wonderful place to raise a family."

His casual comment caused Alisha a pang of alarm, and she darted a glance at the third finger of his left hand. It was ringless, but she couldn't resist asking, "Family? Are you married?"

He smiled, white teeth flashing. "Nope. 'Free, white, and twenty-one.' I had my brother's children in mind."

"Never have been married?" she persisted.

"Not even once." The laugh lines radiating from the corners of his eyes etched deeper. "Furthermore, I have no intentions of ever changing my status."

Before she could pursue the subject, the waitress was at their table, order pad in hand. "What'll you have?" The young woman couldn't have been much younger than Tammy, but she was obviously dazzled by Zach, and Alisha noticed a dimple that deepened with the radiant smile she bestowed on him.

Preoccupied with this reaction and with the strange retort he had made earlier, Alisha gave her order absently. "Just a Sprite, thanks."

Zach studied her expression with a quizzical look. "Sure you won't have something more? Supper was hours ago, and walking works up an appetite." Alisha firmly refused. "Then bring me a banana split," he said to the goggle-eyed waitress. "I'll try to force a few bites on this young lady."

"Be right back." The girl moved off with an expression of adoration and a swish of her ponytail, leaving the two sitting in an uncomfortable silence.

"This place brings back memories," Alisha said, casting about for a safe topic of conversation. "It reminds me of a restaurant where my grandfather used to take us years ago, when we visited him in the country."

"Us?"

"My sister and me."

"Somehow I had the idea you were an only child."

"No," she said hesitantly. "I had a sister, but she . . . died."

"That's tough. I lost a brother, too. So I know how it feels."

Alisha did not reply until the waitress had set their orders before them and had left to serve another table, with a lingering look in Zach's direction.

"I'm not sure you do," Alisha said softly and bent her head over her drink, allowing her hair to fall about her face, hiding it from his scrutiny. "How long has your brother been dead?"

"Almost three years now, and I still haven't gotten over it." He gazed off into the distance. "He and I worked on the same boats, took the same trips. He had a heart attack and died one day when we were down near New Orleans. Guess I took the coward's way out . . . just couldn't go back on the river, knowing he wouldn't be with me. So I've been working on the lake steamers ever since. . . . That day I saw you in Buffalo, I was on my way home."

"To stay?"

"Maybe." He shrugged his shoulders. "This summer will give me the feel for the river again. Then, in my off time, Mom needs my help with the farm. She's doing the work of two men."

"What about your father?"

"He died before I was born. I'm the only Martin male—"

The waitress interrupted his story with the check and a coy smile. "Sorry, folks, but we close in five minutes. I'll be glad to take this up for you."

Zach reached for his wallet with a reassuring grin for Alisha. "Guess that's our cue." He peeled off a bill. "Plan to catch the showboat performance tomorrow night?"

"Wouldn't miss it! The whole town's closing down for the evening. It's been a long time since a showboat has docked at Vandalia!"

chapter
5

THE SHOWBOAT SEASON OPENED with a parade through the streets of Vandalia. Dressed in twin outfits of ivory satin decorated with red sequins, Tammy and a young university student led off, while Alisha followed bravely behind with the marching band, blowing a borrowed trumpet. The rest of the cast, in costume, moved at a more leisurely pace, greeting people on the sidewalks and presenting printed flyers giving the details of the performance. By the time they returned to the *Laurel,* Paul felt assured of a sell-out crowd.

As curtain time neared, the butterflies in Alisha's stomach multiplied, and her fingers shook as she put on the Indian wig for the first act.

"Oh, everybody feels nervous on opening night," Tammy assured her with all the confidence of a seasoned professional, though Alisha knew her young friend's only experience consisted of bit parts in a few high school plays.

Still, a peek at the audience through a slit in the curtain served only to intensify her apprehension. The crowd was at capacity, with a few spectators spilling over into the balcony, seated alongside the lights. The pit, immediately below the stage, where at one time an orchestra would have performed, was overflowing with bouquets of flowers donated by the business people of the town. The pungent aroma of roses brought a flood of memories of another day not too long ago, when she had fled in horror at the prospect of what she was about to do. She had an equally disquieting sensation now, and the urge to run was almost overwhelming.

"So there you are." Zach's resonant voice was laced with tenderness and humor. "I was sent to chase down one runaway Indian maiden."

It was as if he could read her thoughts. "Oh, Zach. I don't think I can do it," she murmured. "How did I ever get myself into this?"

"Hey," he tilted her chin upward with his index finger. "You're not alone. We're all together in this and . . . have you forgotten your faith in the Lord? He's with you, too, you know. Now I've got to go turn off that canned music and make some of my own. As the old saying goes, 'Break a leg,' honey."

She ducked her head in embarrassment. "Thanks, Zach. I'd better let Paul know I haven't bolted." She drew a deep breath. "See you in 1749."

She found her place beside Tammy in a makeshift cornfield before a backdrop depicting a primeval forest glowing with autumn colors. A wide river flowed beside the woods.

"Where were you?" Tammy hissed, her black silk braids falling over either shoulder. Even the copper make-up failed to hide the sprinkling of freckles across her nose. "We thought we were going to have to start without you!"

"Tell you later." Alisha fell into her role quickly, working the fertile land with a crude hoe as other actors pantomimed the carefree days of the Indians before the European invasion. She scarcely recognized the students beneath the decorated faces of young braves who entered the serene village with a deer, fresh from the kill, slung across their shoulders.

In the rising tension of the scene, she joined the others in acting out a feast of harvest foods—the recent kill, corn, beans, pumpkins, nuts, and berries. For the moment, she was not a woman of the 1980s, but a nameless Indian, giving thanks for daily bread.

She actually sensed the impending danger when a canoe arrived at the far end of the set, bearing Mike Price, resplendent in bright silk cape and plumed hat. When he stepped from the canoe, he became Pierre Joseph Celeron de Bienville.

Celeron approached the chief of the village and spoke in heavily accented tones. "The King of France has sent me to extend his guardianship over this river and the people of this valley."

In sign language, the chief asserted that the valley belonged to the native Americans, not the French. Over his arguments, Celeron took a lead plate from a wooden chest, and while he made an impassioned speech, his men buried the plate near the river. Near the village, the Frenchmen raised the flag of France, and the canoes moved on downriver.

Alisha found it difficult to shed her Indian role as easily as she plucked the braided wig from her head and stepped out of the fringed burlap dress.

"Boy!" Tammy muttered, pulling on a bonnet for the frontier scene. "That one may have been a snap, but I'm not so sure about this next segment. We have lines to remember this time. Here—" She presented her back to Alisha. "—fasten my buttons, would you?"

"Hey, where's all that confidence I heard earlier?" Alisha joshed her younger friend, but her fingers were trembling as she finished the long row of covered buttons parading down the back of the calico dress. At the sound of a quiet bell, she almost panicked. "It's time to go . . . and I can't remember my first lines!"

But when she stepped into the new scene, settling herself in one of the flatboats that had been constructed to simulate those carrying the emigrants, once more she felt transported to another era.

Feeling like one of those early travelers, Alisha delivered her lines with great conviction as the flatboaters established themselves in a village along the river. Her pulse quickened at the sight of Zach entering stage left to propose to the settlers that they organize a church. Later, as she knelt beside him for the prayer of dedication, she stole a furtive glance at the chiseled profile, and when the scene ended, she left reluctantly for yet another costume change.

"Good grief!" Tammy complained. "Dad will have to give us a bigger room. There's no way we can dress in this closet."

"Oh, we'll manage," Alisha said, tying back her hair with a satin bow to match her dress and coaxing some wispy tendrils to float about her face. "It's just that these hoops take up so much space."

"Wow!" Tammy turned her full attention on Alisha. "You look exactly like Scarlett O'Hara!"

"We'd better get out of here," Alisha advised, blushing slightly under her stage make-up. "There's our cue."

She heard the plaintive sound of Zach's harmonica signaling the change of scenery for the antebellum scene and hurriedly maneuvered her wide hoops through the narrow doorway.

Alisha wandered around on the stage in front of the backdrop, painted to present a bustling dock during the steamboat era. With no lines in these first few moments, she allowed herself the luxury of concentrating on Mike's and Jane's portrayal of a landowner and his wife. The arrival of a packetboat in the river town was her cue for the welcoming speech she had memorized.

Moving as fast as she could in the billowing skirt, Alisha rushed into Jane's arms. "Oh, Mama, I'm so glad you're home. It seems like more than a year since I've seen you. Did you enjoy your visit in England?"

Jane kissed her and Jane replied, "Very much, dear, except we missed you and your sister."

"Did you know there's going to be a war, Mama? I was so afraid you wouldn't get home before it started."

The reunited family moved toward their columned house, discussing the darkening clouds of a civil war hovering over the country.

During intermission, Tammy and Alisha, still wearing their hooped skirts, pushed carts loaded with lemonade and boxes of popcorn and Cracker Jacks through the aisles.

"If you find a token in your box of Cracker Jacks, you'll receive a gift at the close of intermission," Alisha explained repeatedly. Most of the audience received her explanation without question, but one child quizzed, "How come?" as he reached in his box, feeling about with his fingers.

"Because that's how it was done back in the old days." The boy lifted one of the disks triumphantly. "Hold on to that," she instructed, "and in a few minutes, Mr. Blair will call you to the stage for a prize."

According to Paul, the prizes donated by local merchants surpassed the gifts of whistles, toys, and games offered by the old showboats.

When the lights blinked the close of intermission, Alisha followed Tammy backstage to help her dress for the next scene. With her face darkened, Tammy was surprisingly believable as Eliza, the girl who fled from a life of slavery.

Crossing the half-frozen Ohio, she jumped from one

simulated cake of ice to another. Splashing water gave the scene an authenticity that caused Alisha to shiver from her place in the wings. She thought again of the lost underground tunnel and of the misery endured by those long-ago people struggling to win their right to live in freedom. *If I could only find that tunnel, I'd gain something, too,* she mused. *My parents' approval.*

In the last act, Alisha and Tammy performed their panto-mime-singing routine in a showboat replica of the 1900s. Dressed identically in sequined costumes, they admired their images in the small mirror in the dressing room.

"Not bad, huh?" Tammy said with pleasure. "I knew the first day I saw you we'd look good together. You're so tiny and dark, and I'm . . . just a long-legged redhead." She made a face at Alisha's giggle. "What do you say? Let's go professional when the summer's over."

Alisha shook her head, and the sequined headpiece hovered precariously over her eyes. "Not me," she said firmly, inserting more pins to anchor it in place. "This is fun, but I wouldn't want to spend my life on the stage. As for you, young lady, I have an idea your dad would veto that idea in favor of four years at the university."

At the bell, they scurried out of the room and into their rendition of "Grandfather's Clock," accompanied by Zach, this time on the banjo. A college student, secreted inside a huge, hollow clock, provided a ticking sound, pacing the song. Caught up in the theatrics of the routine, Alisha was pleasantly surprised to hear outbursts of spontaneous applause throughout the many verses of the old favorite. When the clock finally sounded an alarm on the night the old man died, the dramatic finish met with a wave of enthusiastic cheering. And, at the finale, when Tammy and Alisha took their bows, their number proved to be among the most popular.

Backstage, Tammy plopped down on the floor. "Whew! I've changed my mind about going on the stage. I wouldn't live through this every night for all the money in the world. I'm all in."

"The night is still young." Alisha took out the pins and removed the heavy headdress before flipping a brush through her hair. "Don't forget the reception at the River Hotel."

Tammy moaned but allowed herself to be hoisted to her feet.

The ballroom of the hotel, lavishly decorated with summer flowers, was the world of a century earlier. Alisha walked in at Zach's side. Hostesses in hoop-skirted gowns greeted the guests. There was an unhurried elegance in their movements, precipitated in part, Alisha knew, by the cumbersome hoops.

Despite her dread in facing a roomful of strangers, Alisha gave herself over to the mellow mood inspired by the setting and actually began to relax with the friendly townspeople.

The butterflies, in full flight, returned to her stomach when Zach introduced her to his mother. "You two get acquainted while I round up some refreshments," he urged, then promptly disappeared into the throng.

"Well," Mirian Martin began, assessing Alisha with snapping dark eyes, "so you're working with my son this summer." Alisha felt herself growing warm under the woman's intense gaze. "Tell me, are you a student at the university?"

So far, she could handle the conversation. "No, I graduated from a college in New York in May and intend to find a permanent job as soon as the tour ends. As you could tell—" She laughed apologetically. "—I'm really not a performer."

"On the contrary, I thought you gave an excellent performance. The duet with Tammy was outstanding."

Alisha's face flushed with pleasure. "I must admit it's a new experience for me . . . the shows, living with the cast. . . . With only my parents at home, I've never known what it's like to be surrounded by people."

Mirian studied her with what appeared to be sincere interest. "Well, I suppose it does have its disadvantages . . . little privacy—"

"Oh, it's *too* quiet at home!" Alisha insisted, almost too quickly. "I'm certainly not ready to go back."

Mirian laughed softly. "Good. I'm sure you'd be missed if you left. And you might even find that the pleasures of a large 'family' outweigh the inconveniences."

Before she knew it, Alisha was chattering away, telling this woman of her stage fright, her keen interest in history, and how she had surprised even herself in being able to slip so easily into the various parts she had been assigned.

"Maybe it's because I feel more at home in the past than I do in the present."

Just as Alisha was about to confess her secret desire to uncover something of historical significance, Zach returned, carrying a tray of sandwiches and frosted glasses of lemonade.

"Well, here we are, ladies. Sorry to be so long. There's a real run on the refreshments. I had to stand in line."

While Zach chatted with his mother, Alisha munched on a sandwich and considered her own uncharacteristic behavior. She had opened up to Mirian Martin as if she had known her always. What strange power did this woman possess that had unlocked Alisha's deepest thoughts?

Why can't all mothers be like that? she thought and instantly felt ashamed. In the past few days her emotions had swung like a pendulum. One minute she was chiding herself for the way she'd treated her parents; the next, she was resenting them for their lack of understanding. More than once, she'd considered telephoning to let them know that she was safe, but each time, she'd made some excuse not to call.

Regarding Zach and Mirian again, their heads together to hear each other above the din of tinkling china and countless other conversations, Alisha saw that mother and son bore scant resemblance to each other. Still, they shared the same keen brown eyes and outgoing personality.

Alisha hadn't realized she'd been so preoccupied with her own musings until Zach snapped his fingers in front of her face. "Penny for your thoughts."

"Don't waste your money." She laughed to cover her embarrassment.

Mirian handed Zach her plate. "I have to leave now, son. We have a field of tobacco to set out tomorrow." Mirian embraced them both. "You must bring Alisha home with you for a visit when you have time off."

Though the idea had not occurred to Alisha before this moment, the idea of a visit with Mirian Martin intrigued her.

At nine o'clock the next morning, the *Laurel* was on its way south toward Huntington. Zach heralded the departure from Vandalia with a familiar tune on the calliope.

"I'll have to admit, he's improving," Tammy said as she and Alisha waved to the crowds on the bank. A flotilla of motorboats surrounded the showboat to give it a rousing send-off.

After their second performance at Huntington, Paul called the cast together. "I'm predicting a successful summer. You're all to be congratulated . . . and warned. Right now, we're all good friends, but I want it to stay that way. In such close quarters, even the best of friendships can be strained." He paused, and Alisha wondered what was coming next. "To relieve the natural tension," Paul continued, "I'm suggesting a twenty-four-hour leave every ten days for all crew members, two at a time." *Oh, good. Maybe Tammy will be my tour guide.* Alisha's thoughts wandered. "I've made arrangements for my station wagon to be waiting at the next stop. Then, those of you on leave can use the wagon and meet the boat at the next port."

It was a novel idea, Alisha thought, and the entire crew welcomed the chance to do some sightseeing while keeping the performances on schedule.

"Hope you don't mind," came a masculine voice as she stood next morning, scanning the names. Her name and Zach's headed the list of the cast to go on leave.

"So *you're* responsible for this."

"Guilty as charged," he replied with an impudent grin.

She should have been furious, but seeing the mock innocence on his face, one unruly lock of hair spilling over his forehead like a very small boy, she hadn't the heart to scold him.

"It's just that I wouldn't want to start any rumors or—"

"Oh, I'm perfectly harmless, you may be sure. I just thought you might want a qualified guide to the Ohio Valley. After all, I feel responsible for you, since I was the one who advised you to strike out on your own."

"Well . . . we could try it . . . just this once."

Unbidden, her mother's face flashed before her. "Once a girl's good name is tarnished, it's never forgotten." She could even hear the disapproving tone in Ethel DeFoe's voice, but when she voiced her concern later to Tammy, her friend cried, "Good grief! Zach isn't interested in romancing women. He'll treat you like a sister. Go on and have a good time."

Still apprehensive at six o'clock when the boat docked at Greenup, Kentucky, Alisha picked up her suitcase and started reluctantly for the gangplank where she was to meet Zach.

Paul's wife, Roberta, had brought the station wagon to the landing and was in the process of being enveloped in a bear hug—Paul, on one side, and Tammy, on the other.

"Mom, I wish you could have come along," Alisha overheard Tammy say. "Dad and I miss you."

"Believe me, darling, there's nowhere else on earth I'd rather be," said the woman when she had caught her breath.

Roberta Blair was a stunning blonde with silver tinging the hair at her temples, Alisha noticed, nothing at all like Tammy, who took after her father in appearance.

"But you know Grandma Sullivan isn't well, and I need to be with her." Her voice was a melodious blend of West Virginian and midwestern, Alisha guessed. "We'll make up for it when we do get together, I promise. Besides, I'll just bet Ma is spoiling you with her good cooking. You know I don't hold a candle to her in the kitchen."

At that, the stout older woman rushed off the boat to greet her daughter-in-law. Alisha could not believe her eyes. Families just didn't display such feelings openly up north.

Zach opened the door, and Alisha slid silently into the seat of the station wagon. "Why so quiet?" he said, as they drove away from the landing. "Not having misgivings already, I hope."

"I was just thinking about the Blairs' reunion . . . at the dock back there. I'm afraid I'm jealous."

"Love is the key," Zach said as he reached for her hand and squeezed it.

"I suppose my parents love me, but they've never said so in so many words. Even when I told them I didn't love

Theodore and wanted to call off the wedding, they seemed to think I was being hopelessly naïve."

Zach's voice was unexpectedly sober. "A word of advice. Don't ever marry unless you love the person so much you can't help yourself." Then he smiled broadly. "But let's put Buffalo behind us for the time being and concentrate on having a good time."

She was more than willing to comply. "Any recommendations?"

"Only that we'd better find a place for the night, first thing. During the tourist season, good hotels are hard to come by." He slanted her an appraising look before continuing. "Someone told me about an old stagecoach inn that has been converted into a hotel. Since you're so interested in history, I thought you might like to stay there."

"Well . . . I suppose so." Suddenly, the idea of spending some time with this thoroughly likable, thoroughly non-threatening young man was surprisingly pleasant. She decided to enjoy herself. "Yes, I'd like that very much."

After an inquiry at a service station, Zach had no trouble finding Bolton Tavern, which stood in a grove of tall trees, far enough from the busy highway to ensure quiet and privacy.

The native limestone building had been built in 1800 to serve the stagecoaches running from Pittsburgh to Louisville, they learned. The upper story had originally been divided into ten rooms, with separate quarters for men and women.

Alisha blinked at the cost of the room, but the price did include dinner and breakfast, and when Zach asked her opinion, she agreed that this was a bargain.

"It's charming!" she exclaimed when the bellman opened the door of her room and deposited her luggage on the floor.

Antiques gave the room a homey feeling, and a bright quilt, likely pieced at some local quilting bee, adorned the bed.

67

Varnished to a shine, the wooden floor of wide planks displayed three round rag rugs beside the half-canopy bed and in front of the dresser. Hand-hewn beams and whitewashed walls set off the colonial decor.

Zach, who had looked in from the hall, cast an appreciative eye around. "If you like antiques," he commented, "you'll love Cedarpoint."

"Cedarpoint?"

"My home. I grew up with furniture like this." He glanced at his watch. "The manager said dinner would be served at seven o'clock, so that doesn't give us much time. Shall I knock on your door in a half-hour?"

She smiled. "Just time enough to shower and change."

"Don't doll up too much. This place is pretty quiet and unassuming."

Alisha closed her door with a light heart, humming one of the show tunes. She hurried through her shower and pulled out an ivory knit that was a part of her trousseau.

Mother always did have good taste, she thought, sliding the dress over her head and arranging it over her hips. Checking her reflection in the mirror, she decided that the neckline of the surplice bodice wasn't too low, and that the exquisitely embroidered lace top did do something for her complexion. She pulled on a pair of high-heeled sandals.

While she waited for Zach to arrive, Alisha looked out over the rolling green hills of lush pastureland and wondered if the area had changed much since Daniel Boone's first visit to the region.

When she opened the door at the sound of Zach's knock, she found that he had exchanged his jeans and crewneck for white twill trousers and a burgundy shirt.

His eyes lit up when he saw Alisha, and he whistled. "Well, hello, Princess," he said, as if he had never seen her before.

"Are you sure I'm in the right room?" He checked the number on the door. "Same room, all right, but you have certainly undergone a transformation."

"Oh, don't be silly," Alisha told him as she locked her room and dropped the key into his pants pocket. "This was the only dress I brought with me."

Well, tonight, if he thought she looked like a princess, she'd oblige him. "Lead on, Sir Galahad." She played along, dropping a small curtsey before preceding him down the stairs.

Once the tavern's taproom, the spacious dining area was papered in a scrolled reproduction design that complemented the walnut woodwork. A young woman in colonial dress led them to a table, and Alisha felt again that she had been thrust backward in time. Candles flickered on the tables, and a costumed matron played an antique pump organ.

Alisha's eyes glowed, and Zach watched as she looked around the room. "I've never seen anything like this before," she whispered, as if speaking aloud would shatter the illusion. "My parents prefer posh *new* eating places."

The waitress laid a menu before them and soon returned with glasses of ice water. Some of the entrées were new to Alisha, so she said to Zach, "Please order for me."

"The aged Kentucky ham for the lady, and I'll have the roast venison." He winked at Alisha. "If the ham's too salty for you, we'll switch."

Though pungent, the meat was delectable, and Alisha even tried a bite of Zach's venison, though she cringed to think she could actually eat an animal with such trusting brown eyes.

"Then how do you ever manage a good piece of prime rib?" teased Zach. "If anything, cows' eyes are even bigger and browner."

The vegetables—corn pudding, baked squash, turnip

greens, and hash-brown potatoes—were served family style, along with feather-light spoonbread.

Zach ate with obvious relish. "This is southern cooking at its best—the kind I grew up on."

"Hmmm. These dishes are all firsts for me," Alisha confessed, "but I must admit they're quite tasty . . . with the possible exception of . . . this one." She held up a forkful of the stringy dark greens. "This looks like some kind of weed."

"Spoken like a true city gal." Zach chuckled, and the rich sound of his voice fed the hungry place in her heart. "You're something, you know that? I like a woman who's game for new experiences."

"Who? Me?" She turned wide eyes on her dinner partner. "The original Nervous Nellie?" She dropped her gaze and toyed with her water goblet. "I do enjoy learning about the way things used to be, though. It seems times were simpler then, the people more . . . real."

"Ah, Alisha—" Zach looked at her with a curious mixture of humor and affection. "—don't you know that, except for the transforming power of Christ, people never really change? They're still pretty much the same, no matter what historical era they happen to be born in."

"But the Blairs are different . . . and you . . . I've never met anyone like you."

"Oh, I'm not so special. There are some regrets. Education, for one. After high school, I chose to work with my brother John on the river rather than go to college. Mom encouraged me to study business administration. Said I should prepare myself to manage the family holdings someday. . . . Now I wish I had."

His look of dejection elicited a sympathetic nod from Alisha. "Father always wished for a son to take over his business, too, but there was only Carol and I. That's how I almost married Theodore. The merger Father was negotiating with him included *me*."

"Wonder if the business deal fell through after you ran away?"

"I don't have any idea, and I really don't care." She shrugged. "Frankly, I'm having too much fun to give it much thought."

"Then you won't mind being my buddy this summer?" he inquired with a lift of his brow.

She flashed a smile. "I can put up with it, I suppose, especially if this evening is a sample of what's to come. Thanks, Zach." Her voice grew unexpectedly soft. "For tonight . . . for everything."

"Then—" He leaned forward. "—as one buddy to another, don't you think you should let your parents know where you are?"

The languorous smile disappeared from Alisha's face, and she thrust her chin forward defiantly. "No. You don't know my mother. If I contacted them, my folks would be down here immediately, and that would end my plans for the summer."

Zach was incredulous. "But you're a grown woman. Isn't it time you had an understanding with your parents? Why do you let them intimidate you?"

Alisha hesitated, aching to tell someone—anyone. "I told you my sister died. . . ." she began. "I've always thought my mother blamed me for her accident . . . maybe even wished it had been me instead of Carol. . . . It's hard to put into words, but your message Sunday morning helped so much . . . that part about being set free."

"Yes, you told me." His eyes burned with a dark fire, both warming her and prodding her on. "When Jesus sets us free, we are 'free indeed.' No one can hold us captive again."

71

"Maybe, but I'm afraid my parents would try. You couldn't possibly understand what it's like, Zach . . . to be imprisoned by a memory . . . and then to break free. I'm so afraid to go back . . . afraid of losing this beautiful feeling I've found."

She stared, unseeing, into the candle on the table, her eyes catching the dancing light of the flame.

Then take your time, little 'Lisha. Take your time. Zach did not intrude into her private thoughts, but sat quietly as the candle burned low. *You'll know when it's time to go home.*

Once Alisha had been delivered safely to her door, and he had stepped inside his own room, Zach admonished himself. "Watch what you're doing, Zachary Martin. You're dangerously close to falling in love with that young woman, and she doesn't deserve that kind of pain."

He buried his head in his hands. "You aren't her savior, and you don't intend to marry her, so why are you trifling with her?"

In the stillness of the night, the melancholy call of a whippoorwill echoed the loneliness of his heart. He turned abruptly and slammed his fist against the closed door.

chapter
6

THE NOISY CHIRPING OF A ROBIN outside the window aroused Alisha, and she stretched, trying to reach the canopy with her hands. Impossible. *Either I'm too short, or the canopy is too high,* she mused. She closed her eyes, courting sleep again, but it was no use.

Sighing, she reached for her watch on the nightstand. Only six o'clock.

From her window, Alisha could see an inviting expanse of green fields. This would be the perfect time to take a walk. Hurriedly, she donned jeans and a blue plaid shirt, then tugged on socks and jogging shoes.

Leaving the inn wasn't as easy as she had anticipated, for the heavy wooden door was bolted from the inside, and she had to exert all her strength to dislodge and shove the bolt aside before opening the door.

Outside, Alisha headed toward the large grove of trees to the right of the inn, taking advantage of the uneven stones laid to form a walk. Clumps of iris sparkled with dew drops, catching errant rays of sun penetrating the morning mist. Beyond the iris lay a rose garden, and Alisha stooped to smell a saffron bud, glimmering proud and beautiful on its tall straight stem. Not much scent to the rose, but as she sniffed,

Alisha seemed to inhale all the fragrance of the morning. Ironic, she thought, when only short weeks ago, the very thought of roses was stifling.

It had rained during the night, and when Alisha entered the deep woods, she paused for a moment to listen to the plink of lingering drops. Through the heavy foliage, beams of sunlight sought out moisture-laden leaves, turning them to burnished gold. Amber light streaked vivid against the brownish-green forest.

Awed, Alisha stood gazing at a circular spider web, heavy with drops of dew spotlighted by the sun and looking for all the world like a lacy cape encrusted with rhinestones. Suddenly, the clear, sharp call of a cardinal broke the stillness of the morning. When the last note of his song died on the crisp air, she clasped her hands together, feeling God's presence.

The freshness of the dawn coupled with her newfound spiritual freedom lent wings to Alisha's feet, and she bounded through the grove of trees. Grouse scattered at her approach, red squirrels ran for the safety of the trees, and bluejays scolded noisily. Not until she emerged from the woods at a small lake did she halt her stride. Her sudden appearance startled a pair of Canada geese, and Alisha lifted her head to watch them soar into the air, circle the lake, and fly toward the river.

Breathless, Alisha sank onto a fallen log at the edge of the lake. Cattails harbored a flock of mallard ducks bobbing for food, and she smiled at the ducklings gliding close behind their parents. One of the ducklings, boldly following their example, bobbed under the water and remained, upended, for a long moment. Alisha gasped, feeling the sensation of suffocation. Even after the little one surfaced, righted himself, and swam away, an uneasiness settled over her. Wherever she turned, it seemed, she was reminded of the things she most wanted to forget.

The joy of the morning vanished, and she plodded back toward the inn, and sat on a wooden bench that faced the old stone building. A sharp whistle disturbed her somber thoughts. Looking up, she spotted Zach leaning out of his window.

"Early bird!" he shouted. "Don't fly away! I'll be right down!"

"Crazy guy," Alisha murmured under her breath. "He'll wake the whole place, shouting like that." But her smile revealed her pleasure in seeing him. Zach could revive her spirits if anyone could.

She hadn't long to wait, for soon he was sprinting down the stone walkway, and her heart tumbled crazily at his approach.

The dark eyes were slitted against the strong sun, but white teeth gleamed between parted lips. His lithe build was enhanced by white shorts and a striped shirt and he, too, was wearing jogging shoes. Upon closer inspection, Alisha could see that he had trimmed his beard closely and that it seemed to caress the angular planes of his face.

If this had been the man waiting for me at the altar instead of Theodore, I wouldn't have run away. Alisha's senses reeled with the impact of the thought.

She noticed again the fine laughter lines etching the corners of his eyes and longed to trace them with her finger. "Is it insulting to a man to ask his age?" Alisha kept her voice light.

"If you're asking, I've already told you," he said, evading the question. She marveled at the clean, molded contours of his mouth when he formed the words. "I'm 'free, white, and twenty-one.'"

"Humph! Twenty-one plus quite a few, I'd say."

"How does thirty-two sound?"

"Old."

He cuffed her affectionately on the downy curve of her jaw. "Well, all of us can't be wet behind the ears." *Why does she have to look so adorable in the morning?* He clenched his teeth. *Steady, old man. Easy does it. Just friends from now on.*

"Seriously, how did you manage to escape some woman's wiles for this long?"

"Haven't we had this conversation before?" He eased himself away. "Marriage isn't in my plans."

"But why?"

Zach stood and drew her to her feet. "Nosiness doesn't become you." He said it jokingly, but with finality.

Men are peculiar creatures, she thought testily. An hour ago, she couldn't have cared less about Zach's marriage plans, but now it mattered. It mattered a great deal.

"Let's go eat breakfast," he said, interrupting her brooding. "I've discovered the perfect thing for us to do today. Ever been to an auction?" he asked as she walked beside him along the narrow walkway.

"You mean where people buy items that go to the highest bidder?" At his nod, she continued, "No, I've been to flea markets and garage sales, but never to an auction."

"According to a poster in the lobby of the inn, there's an estate auction nearby, starting at ten o'clock. That would give us plenty of time to spend a few hours there and still arrive at Portsmouth by the time the *Laurel* docks."

After breakfast Alisha changed hurriedly. Although intended for a Bermuda cruise, the pink pincord culottes and matching knit blouse should do quite well for a day in the country.

Zach had settled their bill by the time she came downstairs, but she insisted on paying her share. He accepted the money without argument.

"The auction is at an old farmhouse about twenty miles

from here," he said, loading the luggage in the rear of the station wagon before tucking her into the front seat.

Alisha turned for a last look before Zach maneuvered the wagon westward onto the main highway. *What a peaceful place to spend a honeymoon,* she thought, wishing devoutly she could put the idea of marriage—anybody's marriage—out of her mind. There had been a marked difference in Zach's attitude since their discussion this morning, and she had begun to feel her old inferiority complex rearing its ugly head. *Maybe he's having second thoughts about spending his free time with me.*

To her infinite relief, Zach's sunny personality resurfaced as they cruised along the highway, and she plied him with questions about the auction.

"How does it work? What do we do when we get there? Do you think we'll find anything we want to buy?"

"Hold it!" He chuckled, and she felt the old Zach returning. "One question at a time. Auctions are fun even if you don't buy anything—*especially* if you don't buy anything. And we'd better not buy much. I can see Paul's face if we return to the *Laurel* this evening with a bunch of junk." He grimaced at the thought.

"When we get to the place, we'll walk around first and see what's available. Most of the items will be displayed outside on tables or on the ground. The proprietor at the inn mentioned that the property belonged to an elderly woman named Sprague, who had no heirs. There will probably be a lifetime's accumulation for sale, so this should be interesting."

They drove in silence for another half-hour, lulled by the hum of the engine and the hypnotic effect of the bright sun reflecting off the hood of the car. A crude sign announcing, "Auction, 5 miles," was Zach's cue to turn off the interstate.

The unpaved road they took wound uncertainly through

the countryside, the forest pushing in like some bizarre creatures bent on engulfing their vehicle.

When Alisha complained about the jouncing, Zach shrugged off her comments. "No problem. I'm an old hand at country roads. You oughtta see the one to Gran's house."

"Gran? You mean Ma Blair?" Alisha asked as she braced for yet another bump in the road.

Zach slowed a bit and eased the station wagon over the uneven terrain. "No, my Grandmother Crawley. My grandparents live in a log cabin built by the first Crawley to cross the Appalachians. They're in their eighties now and still work like teenagers. You'd like Gran and Grandpa. I'll take you to see them someday."

At least he had no plans to call off their summer treks, Alisha reasoned, and she faced the day with a lighter heart.

"What a shame!" Alisha said when she first glimpsed the old Sprague farmhouse. Unpainted weatherboarding, sagging shutters, and a dilapidated picket fence reminded her of ghost towns she'd seen in movies. "How sad that no one cared enough to keep this place up."

"Yep, it's sad," Zach agreed as they walked among the tables displaying the old woman's treasures. There were dishes, linens, cooking utensils, furniture, and tools.

One table was loaded with stoneware jars, jugs, and crocks. Zach pointed out a three-gallon churn and a gallon jug marked "A. P. Donaghho, Parkersburg, West Virginia." "This blue-stenciled stoneware was made in our state. There used to be several stoneware industries up near Parkersburg, but most of them closed down in the early 1900's."

"Oh, look!" Alisha rushed to six quilts hanging on a clothesline. "That's the Sunbonnet Sue pattern. My grandmother made one of those for both Carol" her voice faltered, but she rushed on "and me." She refused to let thoughts of

Carol ruin the day. She lovingly fingered the appliquéd blocks of small girls dressed in sunbonnets arranged among squares of blue material. "I don't know what these other quilts are called. Do you?"

"I'm not much of a connoisseur of quilts," Zach said with a laugh. "I recognize those two, a Bow-Tie and a Flower Garden." He indicated two multicolored coverlets. "I have some like them on my bed at home." He wandered on. "I know more about furniture. Here's an old piece—a pie safe."

Alisha looked with interest at the four-shelved pine chest enclosed with two doors. The front and sides of the cabinet had tin panels, with a star design punched in the tin.

"The colonial housewives stored their pies in these. The holes gave enough air circulation to prevent mold and spoilage," Zach explained.

"These pink dishes are pretty." Alisha picked up a translucent plate with a rose pattern around the border.

"That's depression glass. It was common back in the 30's, but it's rare now. This seems to be a full set—should sell pretty high."

"I feel like an intruder . . . almost as if we shouldn't be here, ogling the things that were precious to that poor old soul." Alisha picked up a large framed picture of a young woman of a century ago. "Some family member would surely want this . . . but Mrs. Sprague must have outlived them all. It's tragic to be the last of the family line, isn't it?"

"Maybe . . . but I think I'd prefer that to dying young."

Something in his tone caught Alisha's attention, and she glanced at Zach, but he was examining some antique lamps and his expression was inscrutable. *Me and my big mouth!* she berated herself. He was likely thinking of his brother's premature death.

They came to a table loaded with boxes of musty old books. "Just what I've been needing to while away my 'leisure' time on the *Laurel*." She laughed at her own joke. "But I *am* tired of reading nothing but scripts. What do you think these books would be worth?"

Alisha sensed watchful eyes. At her remark, a man who had been pawing through the boxes, turned to give her an appraising glance. Startled, she looked up.

Unkempt hair hung in lank strands beneath a brown cap pulled low over the man's forehead, and his eyes reminded her of a blue shirt that had gone through the bleach cycle too many times. He muttered an obscenity and shuffled away.

Though this brief encounter had left her oddly shaken, Alisha picked up one of the books and leafed through its pages, noting the rather recent copyright date. The title was unfamiliar to her, and she laid the book back in the box and picked up another. She missed her library at home; these would do nicely.

"Look at this." Zach pointed out a large Bible lying on the table. Thumbing through, he paused at a lavishly embellished page in the center. "I'm beginning to wonder about these people," he said. "Apparently, no one bothered to keep the family records, either."

Walking toward an area of the yard cluttered with old furnishings, Alisha tugged on Zach's arm. "See that man? What's he doing?"

It was the same fellow who had examined the books so intently. Now he was inspecting a chest, pulling out each drawer and feeling along the interior and dove-tailed joints.

"Oh, he's probably harmless." Zach shrugged aside her concern. "He may think the old woman stashed a fortune somewhere, and he's determined to find it. From the looks of this place, though, I seriously doubt it."

The bidding began, and the groups of people who had been wandering from table to table gathered around the auctioneer. Zach bid on some old farm tools for his grandfather and won. Alisha stationed herself protectively near the boxes of books in anticipation of her turn.

The auctioneer held up one of the books. "We'll take a bid on one box, and the high bidder can choose any or all of the books at that price."

Following Zach's instructions, Alisha held up her card as the bidding began, but to her surprise it did not end with the fifteen dollars she had allotted herself.

"Twenty dollars!" cried the man with the faded blue eyes. "And I'll take every box on the table."

Dumbfounded, Alisha watched as the man loaded the boxes in a wheelbarrow and trundled them off to his truck. "Well, of all the nerve!" she said, staring after him in disbelief. "Surely, he could have spared a few."

"That's the way auctions go, honey." Zach put a comforting arm around her shoulders. Together, they began to weave their way through the crowd.

"Wait up, young lady!" At the auctioneer's voice, Alisha turned around. "Seeing as how you had your heart set on those books, I thought you might be glad to know I've found another box under the table here. What'll you bid?"

"One dollar!"

When no one challenged her bid, the auctioneer rapped sharply on the table with a small gavel. "Sold for one dollar to the young lady who likes to read! And since you was so patient," the kindly man continued, "I'll throw in this family Bible. 'Pears to me you've got yerself a bargain, with the Good Book into the deal."

Alisha's beam of triumph was accompanied by Zach's yelp of delight. "Now, where else could we have so much fun for so little money?" he asked, shifting the Bible and some of the other books into his box to even the load.

They laughed all the way to the car, staggering with exaggerated emphasis under the weight of their purchases.

"Lady! Lady!"

They turned in unison to see he book buyer laboring after them. "Lady," he puffed, "I'll pay you double your money for that box of books!" He gasped out the words, panting for breath.

Alisha was indignant. "Just how many books can one person read?" she demanded. "You have all the others. Who are you anyway?"

"Cedric Sisson, a collector of rare books. I only want to look through them, and then I'll return them to you."

Alisha glanced at the titles on top. A few Reader's Digest condensed books, some old paperbacks—

"There's nothing here that should interest you. Besides, I bought them, and I plan to read them."

He grabbed at the box. "Ten dollars!" he called as if the bidding were still taking place.

Alisha jerked the box from his grasp and stepped closer to Zach.

"You heard the lady." Zach's voice took on an ominous tone. "The books are not for sale."

"Twenty dollars!" Sisson called as they headed for the station wagon, but they ignored him.

"What's the matter with him?" Alisha wanted to know. "Why is he so determined to get his hands on my books?"

She handed the box to Zach and watched while he loaded it beside the box of tools, then slid into the front seat. In the distance, she could see Sisson, scribbling something in a notebook.

"He was probably telling the truth . . . though if he found a rare book, you can bet he wouldn't return it," Zach said, slamming her door and running around to the driver's side. "The guy looks familiar, though. In fact, I think I've seen him somewhere in the past few days. Well, no matter." He turned the key in the ignition, and the car purred to life. "Let's forget the whole thing."

"It's going to be hard to go back to a routine after today, isn't it?" Alisha sighed. "I don't know when I've had such fun."

"Glad to hear it." Zach kept his eyes on the winding, rutted road, but his lips curved in a smile. "I guarantee you a summer to remember . . . this is just the beginning."

By the time they arrived in Portsmouth, the *Laurel* had docked.

Paul intercepted Zach and Alisha as they carried their purchases on board. "What have you two been up to?" he demanded. "Oh, don't tell me. Let me guess. You found an auction somewhere."

"Take it easy," Zach said with a laugh. "Alisha's books will only take up a little corner of her cabin, and I'll stow my tools aboard the *Susie M* until I can take them to the farm."

By the time showtime rolled around, Alisha's fears that her interlude with Zach might have caused her to forget her lines in the show were quickly laid to rest. On the contrary, her performance that night was even better than before, proving Paul's point in giving the cast an occasional shore leave.

With the busy schedule following their return, however, there was no time to browse among her books. It was three nights later, while Tammy was away, that she curled up on her bunk, the box of books on the floor beside her. She counted twenty volumes, mostly fictional works, but at the bottom of the box was a book entitled *Mysteries of the Appalachians,* with a copyright date of 1890.

Intrigued by the title, Alisha leafed idly through the book. The chapters dealt with lost rivers and underground caverns. In the middle of a yawn, she came to the last chapter entitled, "Lost Underground Tunnel," with the subtitle, "Unusual Art

Exhibit Eludes Archeologists." She sat straight up in bed, instantly alert. Could this be the tunnel the black woman at the library had been referring to?

"Anyone who has casually strolled along the banks of the Ohio River," Alisha read, "may have walked over one of the lost treasures of the art world."

Quoting an ex-slave, the author painted a grim picture of the plight of many Negroes of that day. Once, the slave had hidden in an underground tunnel near the Ohio River. For twenty-four hours, he had waited there for someone to row him across the river to safety.

"Jes' 'bout the time night is comin' on, my two frien's and me, we comes to a white man's place. We been tole to look for a North Star scratch right into the brick on the wall 'bove a po'ch that runs along the front of the house. When we fines it, we knows we's at the right place. Mos' times, the window shutters is open so's to hide the markin's, but when runaways is 'spected, the white folks close 'em.

"We tiptoes, quiet-like, 'round the house 'til we fines a door op'n. Then we skitters down some steps 'til we comes to another door. We tap right sof' two times, wait, then tap agin. But nobody comes, so we jes' push on through.

"We's so tired we caint stan' up, but jes' falls on our knees and eats the food waitin' fer us. They is a few candles in the place, and when I looks 'roun, I sees pi'tures painted all up and down this long tunn'l.

"I sees a man-o'-wah unloadin' darkies at a boat dock in Virginny. I sees mo' slaves workin' in tobaccy and cotton fiel's. I sees a massuh an' missus stan'in' in the ya'd with they house suhvants.

"But my frien's and me, we's goin' to cross the ribber. Ain't no white mens ever goin' to boss us agin'. We's goin' to be free! Free!"

Alisha didn't put the book aside until she had finished the last page. Haunted by the tale she had read, she fell asleep to dream of the unfortunate blacks who had passed through the Ohio Valley on their way to freedom.

The next morning, it was Zach, not Paul, who piloted the *Laurel* from the landing and into the deeper channel of the river. Alisha stood by, admiring the flexing of his muscular arms as he turned the wheel with the finesse of a veteran river man.

It was still a half-hour until rehearsal. Time to ask the question begging for an answer since the wee hours of the morning. "Have you ever heard of a tunnel decorated by fugitive slaves during the days of the Underground Railroad?" she ventured.

Zach laughed. "Never have. Where'd you hear something like that?"

"In one of those books I bought at the auction—there's a whole chapter about it!" Her eyes sparkled with animation. "The tunnel ran from a brick house down to the riverbank, where the slaves waited to be ferried across."

"And I suppose you think you're going to find it?"

Alisha felt her face warming. "Someone will . . . why can't it be me?"

With a blast of her whistle, the *Laurel* greeted the *Roberta Blair* pushing several barges loaded with scrap iron, and Zach gave his full attention to negotiating the waves generated by the towboat. A man working on one of the barges caught Alisha's eye. He seemed vaguely familiar, but, preoccupied with her thoughts, she quickly forgot all about him.

"Now listen, honey," Zach said after the successful passage, "I just don't want you to get your hopes up. It's been well over a hundred years since the Underground Railroad operated through here. If there were such a tunnel, it would have been washed away long ago. The dams and locks have raised the water level of the streams until any opening would have long since been flooded. Then, too, erosion has eaten away at the banks." He looked dubious.

"But surely there must be a few places where the shoreline is unchanged," she persisted.

With a wave of his hand, Zach acknowledged the fact. "Oh, sure. A few towns have built retaining walls, and some of the farms have done the same thing. In fact, my grandfather built a wall at Cedarpoint to retard erosion around our place, but there aren't many. Nope," he insisted, maneuvering the big boat around a bend in the river, "I'm afraid you're looking at a long shot."

"I find that I'm not as easily discouraged as I used to be," she declared with a stubborn tilt of her chin. "I'm going to look for the tunnel—with or without your help. But—" She paused at the head of the steps leading to the lower deck. "I'd rather have you on my side. If I bring you the book, will you read it?"

"Deal!" Zach agreed, flashing her a smile. "But you may as well know, I think it's a waste of time."

She took the steps with more than her usual enthusiasm. *Something tells me this is going to be fun,* she thought. Maybe they wouldn't find the lost tunnel, but the idea of exploring with Zach was reward enough.

chapter

7

ABOARD THE *LAUREL*, it didn't take long to fall back into the strict regimen. There was a certain satisfaction in knowing that rehearsal would begin each morning promptly at ten, showtime at eight, and that the hours between would be filled with a variety of activities.

Alisha and Tammy bought provisions twice each week, and one day a week, the laundry detail took linens to a coin laundry. The staff was responsible for washing personal clothing on board and hanging it out to dry on the upper deck as they traveled. Often the area around the pilot house contained so many items of clothing flapping in the breeze that Paul laughingly referred to his boat as a "floating yard sale."

Alisha learned to love the nomadic life, viewing each day with anticipation as she awakened to a world shrouded in fog—fog so thick at times that she couldn't see from one end of the *Laurel* to the other. As the sun chased the mist away, there were new sights to see as they cruised the river en route to the next town, the next performance.

The show varied from night to night, depending upon which actors were available. One of the students did a credible job as a magician, and one performed an aerial act on ropes rigged across the stage. There was even a mini-minstrel show, with Zach strumming a banjo in accompaniment to a tap dance routine. And Mike frequently scheduled Alisha to sing "I'm Only a Bird in a Gilded Cage," for which she was costumed in feathers.

By the time the boat neared Vandalia on their swing northward, the entire production had improved considerably, and Alisha was feeling much more confident about her roles. Zach, too, had mastered the calliope at last, and though the music was far from melodious to Alisha's ears, the tunes he played upon arrival and departure had grown familiar and dear to her. Even after several weeks aboard the *Laurel,* she still felt a tingle of anticipation when they docked at yet another port to Zach's rousing "Here Comes the Showboat." Nor did she fail to get a lump in her throat the next morning when they pulled away, hearing the scraping strains of "God Be With You 'Til We Meet Again."

Although no show was scheduled in Vandalia for this stop, there was the sense of homecoming among the cast and crew as they neared the Gallipolis Locks. Alisha had experienced the locking process several times, but each time it was a new thrill.

The procedure required both Zach's and Paul's expertise to steer the large boat through the concrete chambers. They stood by until several coal-laden barges came through going downriver, then Paul eased the showboat into the chamber, the *Susie M.* cautiously nosing the larger vessel ahead. With the two boats safely inside, the massive gates folded slowly inward and locked together with a metallic thump.

Standing on deck, several feet below the wall of the lock, Alisha felt as if she were suddenly imprisoned within a concrete cave. Immediately, however, she heard the gigantic pumps churning water around the sides of the *Laurel* to force the boat upward.

"This gives me the creeps," Tammy said, echoing Alisha's thoughts. "I don't like being penned up."

"It'll be over soon," Alisha replied, remembering the sensation of terror she had known when the *Laurel* had passed through the locks for the first time. For a dreadful moment she had gasped for breath, feeling that she would soon be submerged in an icy tomb. But when the boat reached the top level and slid into the more tranquil waters of the river, she had felt immense relief, and the terror had not returned to plague her.

"We'll be passing my home sometime today," Zach told Alisha several hours later. "When you hear three blasts of the whistle, get to the upper deck. You should have a great view of Cedarpoint from there."

The cast had just finished rehearsal for the night's performance when Alisha heard the warning whistle and hurried to join Zach on the top deck of the *Susie M.*

"There it is!" He pointed with pride. "Built by my great great-grandfather soon after the War Between the States."

Cedarpoint rested on a knoll about a mile from the river. A wide sweeping curve of the Ohio provided the setting for the two-story white house, shuttered in green. A well-kept lawn, sprinkled with tall cedar trees, gnarled oaks, and maples, extended to the river's edge.

"Your great great-grandfather?" Alisha inquired, her arm uplifted to keep her wind-tossed hair from her eyes.

"Yes, five generations of Martins have lived there. Ever since my father's death, Mom has run it by herself. My brother and I didn't have Dad's inclination for farming, so we started working on the river."

"But isn't it a large farm for a woman to handle alone?" Alisha asked, taking note of the corn, hay, and tobacco fields greening along the banks.

"Oh, there are tenant farmers to help out . . . but, you're right. It *is* too much for her, and I'm concerned. In fact—" He drew a long breath and squinted against the bright sunlight. "Sometimes . . . being the only man in the family . . . I feel as if I were being torn in two. Do I stay on the river, or go home and relieve Mom?" Suddenly Zach raised his hand and gestured in a sweeping wave. "There she is now!"

Alisha looked to see a broad-wheeled vehicle lumbering through a cornfield. Apparently, Mirian Martin supervised the farm from the seat of a tractor.

"That structure is near the southern border of our farm," Zach explained, pointing out a brick and pole building near the river. "The current is swift as it rounds this bend in the river, and that old retaining wall prevents erosion."

"How unusual." Alisha was more interested in the building than in the walled riverbank extending for more than a mile.

"The brick part was the residence of the first Martin to live here. When he built the bigger house, he added the two-story pole addition to the old house for drying and storing tobacco."

At the next bend of the river, Cedarpoint was lost to view, and Alisha heard Zach's words close in her ear. "The next time we have shore leave, I want you to go home with me."

"There," Tammy muttered as she placed the last sack of groceries in the station wagon. "I hope we have everything Ma ordered. This grocery-buying detail is getting old."

"Maybe so, but it does give us a chance to look around the river towns," Alisha reminded her friend.

Right now, though, she had the strangest feeling that *she*

was being watched. Making a visual sweep of the parking lot, she could see no movement, no evidence of anyone else about. *You're getting paranoid, Alisha. You've been reading too many weird history books!* she chided herself.

But when she checked the other side of the street, she saw a man leaning against a parking meter, arms crossed, eyes under his slouch cap trained on her. Though she couldn't make out his features, she felt sure he was the same man who had harassed her the day of the auction. She paused, her hand on the handle of the car door.

"Tammy!" Her voice was a hoarse whisper. "Do you know that man?"

Tammy glanced in the direction Alisha indicated. "You mean Old Stringy Hair over there? No, I don't know him," she replied as Alisha slid into the seat beside her, "but I've seen him before. He came to the show a few nights ago."

"You mean, he's been on the *Laurel?*"

"Sure. He's not the first creep we've had in the audience." Tammy shifted gears and reversed the station wagon, then wheeled the vehicle around and moved out into the flow of traffic.

Alisha noticed that the man had disappeared by the time they reached the spot where he had been standing. "Zach and I ran into him in Kentucky. He tried to buy my books at the auction . . . said he collected them."

Tammy gave a snort of derision. "Ha! That man doesn't even look like he can *read!*"

"Well, he makes me uncomfortable. I just wish I knew what he was up to. Do you suppose he's following me?"

"Don't worry about it. He wouldn't dare try anything on the *Laurel*, and Zach will more than likely be around when you're off duty." She gave Alisha a sidelong glance. "Speaking of Zach, I've tried to warn you about him. I wouldn't become too fond of him if I were you."

"Do you know much about him?" Alisha couldn't resist asking. "Do you know why he has avoided . . . marriage . . . all these years?"

"Not really. I just know that he stopped dating a few years ago. About the time his brother died, I think. He's paid more attention to you than he has to any woman for a long time. Serves him right if he falls in love with you." Tammy grinned as she careened around the next corner.

"What do you mean by that?"

"Oh, he's broken plenty of hearts in his time. You know the type. All he has to do is saunter around with that slow grin of his, and the women drop in their tracks."

"What about you?"

Tammy looked startled. "Me? Are you kidding? Alisha, he's *ancient!* Besides, he's my sister's brother-in-law, so that makes us some kind of shirttail kin, I suppose. Sure I love the guy, but I love him like a brother."

Despite her disturbing encounter with the stranger, Alisha returned to the boat with a light heart.

With Tammy and her father scheduled for a visit home, Alisha found herself facing some idle hours. No show was scheduled for the evening, and the *Laurel* had failed to make it through the Racine Locks before nightfall. Now, the boat tarried along an isolated stretch of river.

After supper the students withdrew to discuss class notes, and without the frenzied activity of a production night, Alisha grew restless. She tried to read in her stateroom, but the full moon reflecting off the rippled water through the porthole lured her outside.

Hearing the sound of a guitar from the upper deck, she

mounted the steps. Zach was sitting on a bench near the pilot house, striking the chords absently. She waited, hesitant to intrude on his privacy.

In the past couple of weeks, his attitude toward her had changed noticeably. There was no longer the easy camaraderie between them, no subtle underlying note of excitement—of something deeper than friendship that might, given enough time, ripen into love. On the few occasions when they were thrown together, he had been careful not to touch her, and even a casual contact brought an immediate apology. Why he had become so indifferent and distant she could only guess.

Zach's rich voice caressed the words, "What a friend we have in Jesus." Soft waves lapped against the willows growing along the river, and the distinctive tones of myriad creatures provided a harmonious background for the song.

A few lights gleamed at each end of the *Laurel* and the *Susie M.*, but only the shimmering moonlight illuminated the place where Alisha stood.

Unsure of her welcome, Alisha eased down on one end of the bench. Zach acknowledged her presence with a nod, but continued to sing. When he started the lyrics, "Drifting with the current down a moonlit stream," Alisha joined him.

> Drifting with the current down a moonlit stream,
> While above the heavens in their glory gleam
> And the stars on high
> Twinkle in the sky.
> Seeming in a paradise of love divine,
> Dreaming of a pair of eyes that looked in mine.
> Beautiful Ohio in dreams again I see
> Visions of what used to be.

They ended with the high note of Zach's tenor complementing her own mid-range soprano. He laid down the guitar

93

and moved a little closer. "We sound pretty good together. I'll have to ask Mike to add that number to the show."

Flustered, she stammered, "D—Don't stop because of me. With Tammy away, I didn't have anything to do . . . and it was so lonely out here . . . I mean, so *lovely*—" Her voice trailed away in utter confusion.

"Yep. You're right, there." He placed his arm along the back of the bench, and Alisha waited for his touch. It didn't come. "I've been sitting here trying to decide what to do when the tour ends," he mused. "I'm thinking about going to work on our new boat, which should be ready for operation by September." He turned a lazy grin on her. "You? You made any plans yet?"

Her head was spinning with his nearness. "W—When we stopped at Vandalia," she said, hoping the proper words would come to her, "I dropped by the library. Mrs. Foster said the job was mine in the fall—" Now he was leaning toward her, and his eyes in the mellow light were like dark pools of melted chocolate. *If he comes any closer*— "uh . . . I'll work there . . . uh, that is, if the grant comes through." *What is he trying to do to me? First, he practically stops speaking, and now*—She jumped with the shock of electricity kindled by the touch of his hand on her shoulder. "I—I like . . . Vandalia," she finished miserably.

"Good place for you . . . Vandalia," he echoed.

The next thing she knew she was in his arms, her head cradled between his hands. She could feel the whisper of his breath against her face, the brush of his velvet-soft beard as his lips hovered above hers. She felt like a stringed instrument awaiting the skill of the musician to release a captive melody and closed her eyes in anticipation.

Suddenly, however, she could feel the night chill where the warmth of his body had been, and her eyes flew open. Zach had crossed to the rail that circled the top deck and stood there, balancing his foot on the lower rung and gazing out at the silver river.

Alisha gasped. She was disappointed, shaken, and just plain mad! What was the matter with the guy, anyway? What was the matter with *her*?

Zach made a half-turn, looking at her over his shoulder. "It's late." He spoke as if nothing had happened . . . or almost happened. "We've a long day tomorrow. As soon as Paul pulls in, we'll be heading for Cedarpoint."

"Well, then," Alisha said as soon as she could find her voice, "I'll be saying good night."

She didn't know whether her legs would support her when she stood, but somehow she managed to cover the distance to the narrow steps with some degree of dignity before she fled down them and into her cabin. Then she flung herself, face down on the bunk, her agony too searing for tears.

The moonlight filtering through the porthole brought no peace of mind now. All her old guilt and loss—her parents' rejection, the old pain over Carol's death—came flooding back like the cold, cold waters of Lake Erie so many years ago, overwhelming her with its intensity.

She flipped on the lamp. Tammy's Bible lay on the table, and Alisha clutched it. "Lord," she whispered, "I need you so much. I can't depend on Zach . . . or my parents . . . or even myself. Lord, I need you more tonight than I've ever needed you before. Please . . . tell me what to do."

She thumbed the concordance in the back until she came to the heading of "Security." *Security*. That's what she needed. Seeing a reference to Psalm 27, she turned to it eagerly and read the comforting words: "The LORD is my light and my salvation—whom shall I fear? The LORD is the stronghold of my life—of whom shall I be afraid?"

Did that mean she had nothing to fear? Not rejection? Not the treacherous waters of the Ohio River, or even Lake Erie? Could she really believe that? She read on, her heart pounding with conviction when she came to verse 10: "Though my father and mother forsake me, the LORD will receive me."

But had her parents really forsaken her, or had she forsaken them? Alisha felt a twinge of regret. She had no qualms about having refused to marry Theodore. Her parents were in the wrong about that, but she had been wrong, too. She had no doubt caused them untold anxiety, compounded by the embarrassment of walking out on her wedding.

Contrite, Alisha read on through the psalm. The last verse generated both hope and further questions. "Wait for the LORD; be strong and take heart and wait for the LORD."

Patience wasn't one of her virtues, she thought with fresh shame. She had almost brazenly invited Zach to kiss her just now. Maybe she'd even put temptation in his way, when all he had meant to offer was his friendship. Well, if that were the case, she'd back off. Any woman should be grateful for a friend like Zach.

But there was one thing she could have, and she accepted it at that moment. "For in the day of trouble he will keep me safe in his dwelling; he will hide me in the shelter of his tabernacle." Alisha claimed the promise for herself, snapped off the light, and promptly went to sleep.

Zach crossed to the *Susie M.,* but despite the heavy schedule of the next day, he didn't go to bed right away. Instead, he dropped into a deck chair on the stern of the towboat, his head in his hands. The moon had disappeared over the western horizon before he stirred again.

How can I possibly spend the weekend with Alisha without making a fool of myself? He moaned aloud. *I'm not made of wood*. For a moment he almost regretted having invited her to Cedarpoint but rejected the idea as soon as it was fully formed. He wasn't in the habit of vacillating, and he wasn't about to start now. Still, he needed wisdom beyond his own. While he had always managed to resist attractive females before, Alisha was different . . . very different.

Kneeling on the dewy deck, he prayed, "Lord, I've used all the strength I have. Please help me. I can't make it through this weekend without you."

chapter
8

MIRIAN MARTIN WASN'T AT HOME when Zach and Alisha arrived at Cedarpoint and walked up the fan-shaped steps of the old brick house. But the housekeeper, Ida Stevens, a plump matronly woman, welcomed them warmly as Zach followed Alisha into the central hall.

"Your mother won't be in from the fields for an hour yet," Ida told Zach. "She asked me to put Miss DeFoe in the front west room. Maybe you'd like to show her around before dinner."

"Say," Zach said to Alisha, "you're getting the royal treatment. That bedroom right across the hall from Mom's room is reserved for *special* guests. I used to beg for that room when I was a child, but I was always shunted to one of the back rooms." There was a hint of mischief in his voice.

"I can tell you've been mistreated," she said with a tentative grin. She still wasn't quite sure how to act around Zach after the fiasco of the evening before.

The decision to visit Cedarpoint had stood, however, despite any reservations she might have had, and Zach had actually seemed more his old self when he met her at the gangplank earlier this morning.

Alisha took a leisurely look around the hall, fascinated by

the high ceilings and fine old moldings. And, when the grandfather clock on the second floor landing struck the hour of four, she had to smile. The dulcet tones were infinitely more pleasing than the improvised stage clock used in her performance with Tammy aboard the *Laurel* .

"Come on, then," Zach said, taking her arm. "I'll give you the grand tour before we dress for dinner." Zach turned to Ida. "What time? The usual?"

She nodded. "Six o'clock. And it's roast beef tonight."

"Good old Mom. She knows it's my favorite." He gave Ida an affectionate pat on the shoulder, then led Alisha down the hall to the right.

Styled in early Georgian architecture, Cedarpoint was built around a center hallway, with four rooms downstairs, four rooms up. Each of the eight rooms contained a fireplace.

"Of course, with central heat, we seldom use the fireplaces," Zach explained, "except in the family room."

The floors were oak, some partially covered by Oriental rugs in muted tones, and there was hand-carved mahogany paneling everywhere, extending from floor to ceiling in the dining room. Elsewhere, the paneling ended at four feet, enhanced by lovely old paper covering the walls all the way to the ornate molding around the borders of the twelve-foot ceilings.

Behind the formal living room and dining area across the front of the house was a modern kitchen from which mouth-watering odors were issuing. Opposite the kitchen, Zach showed her a spacious family room with plump overstuffed furniture inviting a chat in front of the huge fireplace. Alisha was quick to notice, too, the wall of bookshelves crammed with hundreds of volumes, and the family photos arranged on a skirted round table.

"Zach, is this you?" she asked, picking up a framed picture

of a lanky teen-ager in a football uniform, sprinting toward the camera with a football under his arm.

"You guessed it." He colored slightly. "You ought to have seen me without all the padding. I was a real string bean. Fortunately, wide receivers need to be lean meat."

Upstairs, Zach showed Alisha her room with adjoining bath. The magnificent tester bed was draped in velvet hangings tied back at the four posts. A crocheted spread, likely the product of some family member's skill, covered the bed. She was entranced.

"And just so you won't forget," Zach teased, pulling aside the heavy window hangings, "your own view of the Ohio."

His own room was typically masculine. A marble-topped dresser and chest matched the antique cherry bed that had been converted from a rope bed into a more comfortable berth with box springs and mattress.

Pointing to a leather-covered trunk in the corner, Zach said, "That trunk belonged to the first Crawley to cross the Appalachians before the Revolutionary War. He came here from Scotland originally, so I suppose he brought the trunk with him. I prize that old piece . . . for sentimental reasons, I suppose."

"Something to hand down to your children?" She cast him a wondering glance in time to see the mobile mouth contract into a thin line and a slight frown mar the chiseled forehead.

"To my *brother's* children," Zach replied firmly, then continued on a more relaxed note. "There's quite a difference in the backgrounds of the Martins and the Crawleys. The Martins accumulated some money, but the Crawleys placed their values elsewhere."

"When did you say your father's people came to this area?"

"My great great-grandfather Martin brought his family here from eastern Virginia a few years before the Civil War." He picked up a tattered old Bible, strapped with leather, and ran his fingers reverently over the binding. "He opposed slavery, and had a premonition that war couldn't be avoided because of it. So even though he had planned to move to Ohio, when he saw these fertile acres, he couldn't resist settling right here." He replaced the Bible and gazed out over the lawn sweeping down to the river. "Who knows? Maybe he did more for the cause of freedom by staying here in this slave state and using his influence to help the area separate from Virginia and the rest of the Confederacy."

Mirian's arrival interrupted their conversation. "Please forgive my appearance and my not being here to greet you, dears!" The lovely woman burst into the room, brimming with energy and high spirits. "We had a few more acres of hay to bale." Even the blue jeans and flannel shirt she wore did not disguise her elegant carriage, and when she removed her wide-brimmed hat, it seemed to Alisha that every hair was in place. She embraced Zach lovingly, then bent to drop a kiss on Alisha's cheek.

"Welcome to Cedarpoint. I hope you'll consider this your home while you're here, my dear. Now, if you'll excuse me, I really have to freshen up before dinner."

"And I must do the same. I have some unpacking to do," Alisha agreed with a warm smile for her hostess.

Zach had mentioned this family tradition and Alisha was glad, once again, for her mother's impeccable taste. One of the trousseau outfits she had brought along should be ideal.

Soaking in a hot tub was pure luxury after the skimpy shower on the *Laurel,* and Alisha used the few moments to ponder what she had seen and felt during her first hour at Cedarpoint. The house, though well over a century old, testified to constant and tender care. It seemed, almost, that the very walls exuded laughter and love, that they had reached out to embrace her, and that she was a stranger no more. Could it be possible, or was her imagination playing tricks? She wondered. Still, she had felt at home right away.

Drying herself with a thirsty towel, she removed from their hangers a black skirt and a Cathay silk rose-beige blouse and slipped them on. Adding a choker of crystal beads, she surveyed her appearance critically. Maybe she was over-dressed. She went down the stairs, a bit apprehensive. But one admiring look from Zach assured her that she had made a wise selection. And Mirian beamed her own approval.

"How perfectly exquisite, my dear. You've brought a rare kind of beauty to this house," she said, pulling Alisha's hand into the crook of her arm and tucking her own hand into Zach's arm. "Come. Ida tells me that dinner is waiting."

What a pity this beautiful woman is a widow, Alisha thought, admiring Mirian who was sitting at the end of the table, radiant in white lace. Antique diamond earrings dangled against her face, and a diamond choker highlighted her slender neck. Her long black hair swept upward in a bouffant style.

The table was set with translucent china in a dainty gray and white pattern, and sterling silver gleamed against the hand-crocheted tablecloth. Ida had, indeed, prepared a veritable feast—roast beef, mashed potatoes and gravy, corn-on-the-cob, and a medley of fresh vegetables.and gravy, corn-on-the-cob, and a medley of fresh vegetables.

"We raise most of this food here on the farm," Zach told Alisha as he started on his second helping of potatoes. "What's for dessert?" he mumbled, his mouth too full for polite conversation.

"You can't have any dessert until you've eaten everything on your plate," Mirian scolded in the tone she might have used when he was a small boy. "But if you're good, you can have some lemon pie, just the way you like it. I made it myself before I went to the field this morning."

How did she do it? Alisha again marveled at the woman's drive. No doubt she had been up since early morning, first in the kitchen and then, the fields. Tonight she looked every inch a queen, reigning supreme over this banquet table.

"Then you won't have any problem with me, Mom." Zach turned an adoring look on his mother.

Alisha observed this fond exchange under veiled lashes, enjoying the interplay of mother and son as much as the food. She knew that, under the circumstances, she should be feeling like an outsider. Mirian had every right to resent a stranger barging in on Zach's first visit home in several months. But if Mirian minded, she didn't show it.

In the gaiety of his homecoming, Zach's thoughts rioted. If it had been a mistake for him to spend his free time with Alisha, how much more dangerous to have brought her to his home. He cherished the occasional wondering glances she cast as he kidded with his mother and Ida. Her demure countenance when she lowered her curling lashes, so long they almost brushed the downy peach of her cheeks, clutched at his heart. What if she had the right to sit there as his wife? What if she could belong to him forever? The "what if's" stopped there, and with the sheer determination that had disciplined his emotions for several years, Zach turned his attention to the food before him.

"Do you want to be treated like company, or one of the family?" Zach said jokingly as he pulled Alisha's chair back at the end of the meal.

"Oh, I'd much rather be just one of the family," she said with a glance at Mirian, hoping her hostess wouldn't misinterpret her meaning.

"Then let's regroup in the den."

Following Zach and Mirian across the hall to the comfortable room, Alisha perceived for the first time what it was like to be a real family. Never before had she witnessed such a relaxed atmosphere in a home, such genuine love expressed and demonstrated between family members.

Alisha sat silently, sipping the iced tea Ida prepared before leaving for the evening. There was some discussion of farm business, but since Zach kept flashing her frequent reassuring smiles, Alisha felt included, though she didn't understand the first thing they were talking about.

Gazing around the room while they talked, Alisha took note of the pictures on the table near her chair. A double frame held the likenesses of two young men who could have been the same person, except for hair style and clothing. No doubt these were Zach's brother and father. Watching Mirian's face crinkle into spontaneous laughter as Zach's often did, Alisha realized that he bore more resemblance to his mother than to the other male Martins.

"Son, have you gained any new insights into the Scriptures since you've been away?" Mirian was asking, introducing a startling new topic of conversation.

Alisha looked at her, wide-eyed.

"Yes, and I want to share it with you." Zach reached for the Bible lying on the coffee table and turned easily to a portion of the Old Testament. Keeping his finger in the volume, he closed it and turned grave brown eyes on his mother. "For the past year I've been struggling with a decision: Should I leave the lakes and come back here to live?" He opened the Bible again. "Listen to this advice from the book of Isaiah: 'Your ears will hear a voice behind you, saying, "This is the way; walk in it.'"" After I read that, I thought about it for several days."

Zach stood, pacing as he spoke. "I've been as rebellious as

the children of Israel, sulking over my fate and not listening to God's Word when he spoke to me. But I've accepted John's death, Mom. Finally. I should have been happy for him, happy that he's in heaven with Dad. So . . . if you'll have me—" He spread his hands. "—I'm home for good."

Alisha stirred uneasily. She didn't belong here now; these were precious moments that should be shared only by Zach and his mother. She made a move to rise from her chair. "If you'll excuse me, I'll go to bed."

Zach restrained her with a soft touch, and Mirian said quickly, "No need to go, Alisha. There are no secrets here." Alisha slid back into her chair as Mirian grasped Zach's hand.

"Son, you've made me very happy. I haven't prayed that you'd return—simply that you'd find the way to peace of mind and happiness."

"I didn't realize at first, Mom, how selfish I've been, leaving you with all the work and worry. In a way, you not only lost John, but you lost me, too."

Tears glistened in Mirian's eyes, and Alisha felt her own throat constrict.

"The Bible has been my mainstay while you've been away, and one of the most cherished verses is from the book of Job. 'He has caused the widow's heart to sing for joy.' In the midst of my losses, I had the comfort of knowing that a widow's heart can be joyful."

"And I'm going to be here to add to that joy, Mom." Zach's dark eyes sparkled. "I've been thinking of taking out the new towboat in the fall. Paul said it's our turn to come up with a name."

"Well, tonight certainly isn't the time for that," Mirian stated briskly, rising to refill the glasses. "Alisha, forgive us, dear! What must you be thinking? All this shop talk must be so terribly boring."

"Not at all," Alisha protested. "I've loved every minute." When Zach fixed her with a long, level gaze, she felt encouraged to go on. "I'd like to share a verse, too. I'm not a very good Bible student, but I have learned that God will lead one to the right Scripture when it's needed." She glanced appealingly at Mirian. "I don't know what Zach has told you about me."

"Very little . . . but I want to know more."

"Well," Alisha hesitated, "I had some trouble at home and felt it best to get away for a while." She carefully refrained from mentioning that her parents still did not know her whereabouts. "My first night away from home, I was lonely and afraid. Frantic about what I should do or where I should go, I found a verse that has helped ever since. 'Say to those with fearful heart, "Be strong, do not fear.' I'm a real fraidycat," she admitted, unable to meet the serenity in Mirian's dark eyes. At last Alisha lifted her head, squaring her shoulders. "My faith may be weak . . . but God is strong. I'm learning to trust him with . . . everything."

"Oh, my dear girl," Mirian crooned, gathering her into her arms. "You'll find he's always sufficient." Drawing Zach in close, Mirian took his hand and Alisha's, forming a tight circle. "Let's pray before we go to bed."

Alisha felt the warmth of Mirian's concern in her prayer of petition, followed by Zach's strong and confident voice, thanking God for helping him make the decision to come home. When he paused, Alisha's heart accelerated nervously. Did they expect her to join in the family prayer?

Then she remembered the comfort she had received only the night before from her reading of the psalm. "Lord, help me to depend more upon you, less on myself," she prayed. "Help me to accept your plans for my future . . . and I thank you for the love in this home and for the welcome that has been extended to me."

Mirian hugged Alisha and Zach in a single embrace. "You've made me very happy tonight, children."

As they started upstairs to bed, Zach paused at the landing. "Say, I almost forgot Grandpa's tools."

He ran lightly down the steps and out the front door, returning with the box of tools he had bought at the auction in Kentucky. He opened the box to show his mother, and Alisha noticed the old Bible she'd acquired at the sale.

"Oh, the Bible was in your box," she said. "I'll take it upstairs with me."

Zach lifted it gingerly. "It's pretty dusty. Be careful that you don't soil your dress." And to his mother, "I'll put these tools on the back porch, and you can take them to Grandpa when you go out there next time. I think he'll be able to put them to use."

"He'll love them, dear. Thanks for thinking of him. Now, I'm off to bed. I need my beauty sleep." She kissed them again, moved off down the hall to her room, and closed the door behind her.

"If there's anything your mother doesn't need," Alisha mused, staring after Mirian Martin, "it's beauty sleep. She *glows*."

"Yes." Zach's voice was soft. "She's the best. But I know someone else who's pretty special." Brushing a kiss on her cheek, he disappeared into his own room, leaving Alisha standing in the hallway, her hand pressed to the spot still tingling from the touch of his lips.

Sighing, she entered the guest room, set the Bible on a nightstand, and wandered restlessly about the room. She moved from one piece of furniture to another, trailing her hand along the polished grain of the wood. She studied the pictures on the wall, pausing in front of a framed sampler hanging above the chest. Apparently Mirian had embroidered the picture in her youth, for her initials were stitched unevenly at the bottom. But it was the message that caught Alisha's attention. "Love is the master key that unlocks the gates of happiness." She read it over and over.

She readied herself for bed, turned down the coverlet, and plumped the pillows. Then she climbed into the fourposter, sinking down into the feather mattress.

It was useless to turn off the light just yet, she knew. Her mind was still reeling from the events of the day. The Martins had an imposing ancestral home, a position of influence in the community, and were reasonably well off financially, but her parents had most of those things, too, and they weren't happy. No, it was clear to her now just what distinguished the Martins from her own family. Zach and Mirian included God in every facet of their lives. Not only was he their Lord and Protector, he was the very cornerstone of their home.

Reminded of a verse she had discovered recently, she climbed out of bed and tugged the heavy Bible onto her lap. As she opened the pages, she noticed the damaged back cover. It had been repaired with glue. It would need rebinding at some future time—maybe . . . when she got her job with the library.

Paging through the book of Ephesians, she found the passage she had been looking for: "Consequently, you are no longer foreigners and aliens, but fellow citizens with God's people and members of God's household, built on the foundation of the apostles and prophets, with Christ Jesus himself as the chief cornerstone. In him the whole building is joined together and rises to become a holy temple in the LORD. And in him you too are being built together to become a dwelling in which God lives by his Spirit."

Did the *you* in that last verse include Alisha herself? Suddenly she felt a need for God to rule her whole life. She laid aside the Bible, slipped to her knees, and buried her face in the soft bed.

"Lord, you know I haven't really seen any example of personal daily living with you in my parents' lives. The Martins have shown me so much more. Make me a fit dwelling for receiving your Spirit."

Before she went to bed again, she knew the fullness of another prayer answered.

Alisha's step on the stairs next morning was light when Mirian greeted her at the lower landing.

"Zach insisted on taking my place in the hayfield this morning to give us a chance to get better acquainted," the older woman said. "Ida doesn't come in until ten o'clock, so I'm the cook this morning." She led the way into the kitchen. "Did you sleep well, dear?"

"Superbly!" Alisha replied with enthusiasm. "It was marvelous having that huge bed to myself after sleeping in a bunk. Tammy and I manage, but we could set our little cubbyhole in one corner of your guest room."

Mirian laid two plates on the kitchen table and hurriedly prepared their breakfast. Wearing a simple cotton housedress, with an apron tied around her waist, Zach's mother was much less intimidating than the gracious lady who had presided over the dinner table the night before, and Alisha found herself chatting away as she helped dish up their simple meal.

"Will you ask the blessing?" Mirian asked, taking her seat at the round oak breakfast table.

With a sinking feeling, Alisha bowed her head. Mentally she groped for the words Zach and Paul used when they prayed before meals. Finally she murmured a few sentences, wondering later whether they had made sense.

After breakfast they strolled into the family room, much of the conversation centering around the house Mirian obviously loved.

"When I came here as a bride years ago, I was a 'country girl.' This house seemed huge and formidable to me then, for our home out in the hills was small and cozy. All this took a lot of getting used to, but I love it now. When my husband died, I assumed the responsibility of maintaining the place for my sons. Of course, there is only Zach now." For an instant, the lovely dark eyes clouded, but she moved briskly on. "I've tried to keep it in good repair without sacrificing the beauty of the original structure and decor."

"You've been a widow for a long time?"

"Yes, since Zach was a baby. My husband died three years after we were married."

"You're still such a beautiful woman," Alisha said impulsively. "It seems strange that you haven't married again."

Mirian lifted the photograph of her husband, and the tender look on her face revealed more than words. "I have had several opportunities, and a few times I've seriously considered remarriage . . . but once you've been loved by a Martin, no one else will do."

Mirian replaced the photograph on the table and picked up a recent picture of Zach. "Zach is just like his father. He has all the inner characteristics of the Martins—humor, intelligence, ambition, and passion, but he looks like my side of the family. In fact, when Zach is eighty years old, I suspect he'll look exactly like my father."

Mirian sounded as if she were trying to convince Alisha that her son was a fine prospect. *Doesn't she know Zach never plans to marry?* Alisha was puzzled. Perhaps their communication was not as complete as it appeared to be.

"Now that's enough about the Martins," Mirian continued with a smile. "Let's talk about you. What are your interests?"

"I like books, history, old places. . . . Maybe you could help me." Warming to her subject, Alisha explained about the lost museum of the Underground Railroad. "Zach says I'm foolish to think it still exists, that it would have been washed away decades ago. But what about Cedarpoint? It's an old brick house, situated on the river. Is there a basement that could have housed an underground tunnel?"

Mirian shook her head speculatively. "No, it couldn't have been Cedarpoint, although it would have been the kind of thing the Martins would have supported. They hated slavery. But, you see, this house wasn't built until after the Civil War, and there isn't a basement." She tapped her chin reflectively. "Yet there is something familiar about that story. Perhaps I've read the book."

Mirian went to the shelves and surveyed the many volumes. Alisha scanned the titles, too, but didn't find a copy of the book she had bought at the auction.

"Next time, I'll bring you my copy to read." Alisha immediately regretted her hasty presumption of another visit. As yet, there had been no invitation. At least Mirian ignored, or pretended to ignore, the social blunder.

"There may be some connection with our neighbors' farms," she was saying. "A few of them own century-old brick homes, too. I'll check around."

"I suppose I am being foolish," Alisha admitted, her cheeks still flushed with embarrassment, "but at least it gives me something to look for while we're cruising the river."

"I don't think it's foolish at all. Most great discoveries have been made by curious people. If there is such a tunnel, it should be found and preserved." Mirian knelt before a chest in the corner and removed a pair of binoculars. "Take these with you. You'll be able to see the riverbanks much better. And now, I've kept you long enough," she said, getting to her feet. "Zach is in the north field, and he wants you to drive the station wagon over to pick him up. We'll have an early lunch, and you can start back to the *Laurel* afterward."

Alisha drove slowly along the road that gave access to the acreage where Zach was working. She passed a field where a large herd of red and white cattle grazed, lifting their heads to eye her curiously.

She paused to study the tobacco barn. "What is there about that building?" she mused aloud.

Weathered red brick formed the bottom half of the structure, topped by a construction of poles with two-inch spaces between. A tin roof covered the barn—empty now, for Alisha could see through the walls. She must ask Zach, but she supposed the building needed to be open for the drying of tobacco.

Alisha pulled the station wagon to a stop beside a field where Zach was using a hay baler. Periodically, the machine spewed a huge, round bale of hay onto the ground.

When Zach saw Alisha, he shifted down and called a man working nearby to take his place.

Zach strode toward her, his lips parted in a smile that revealed even teeth, dazzling white against his tanned face. Alisha smiled to see the happiness radiating from his very stance. The lithe, lean figure was charged with energy, and at his approach, she drew a sharp intake of breath, watching him with a strange sense of possession.

"Hi, honey!" he called merrily, bringing with him the sweet scent of curing hay. She relinquished her seat behind the steering wheel and slid over to the passenger side. "I've had a great morning!"

"I would never have guessed," she teased and dared to smooth down his tousled hair. "You've even sprouted some hay in your whiskers."

He peered into the rear-view mirror and, with a chuckle, plucked out the offending stalks.

Sobering, he said, "Actually, being here on the farm only compounds my dilemma. I wonder now if I should stay here and manage the farm rather than go to work on the river full-time."

"Can't you do both?" Alisha asked.

Zach started the engine and moved forward. "Not very well. Oh, the farm will be headquarters, and I'll spend every possible minute here. I can help out some, but the responsibility will still be Mom's. Times like these, I'm sorry my great-grandmother decided to expand into the steamboat industry."

"Great grand*mother*? I supposed it was your grandfather who founded the company."

"No, none of the Martin men lived long enough to make many major decisions." He looked her way. "If you don't mind, let's run by the cemetery for a few minutes. I haven't been there since the day my brother was buried."

A chain-link fence enclosed the family cemetery about a mile from the river. Tall cedar trees stood like sentinels around the perimeter of the neatly mown area. A few old graves were marked by distinctive granite shafts, and two graves were covered with concrete.

Zach walked toward the more recent plots. Alisha kept her distance while Zach stood, head bowed, before the newest grave.

Looking about, she read the markers and made some mental calculations.

John Martin	John Martin, Jr.	John Martin, III
Born 1891	Born 1921	Born 1954
Died 1924	Died 1956	Died 1985

Strange that all three men passed away in their early thirties, Alisha thought and moved away quietly to leave Zach to his grief.

From the edge of the cemetery, she could see the Ohio River in the distance, while nearer, neat rows of corn shifted sinuously in the wind wafting toward them from the west.

Zach's silence continued as they left the cemetery, and Alisha could sense his sorrow. She longed to ask him if his mourning were tinged with the kind of guilt she felt over the death of her sister, but she could not bring herself to discuss, even with Zach, that deep sorrow.

Alisha reached out and touched Zach's arm in a comforting gesture. He moved his head from side to side as if to shake off the past.

"I want to thank you for sharing this part of your life with me," she said. "I know a stranger like me shouldn't have intruded on your first visit home in months, but both you and your mother have been so gracious that I haven't felt like an outsider."

"An outsider!" Zach cried, and he stopped the car under a giant oak tree spreading its shade across the road not far from the tobacco barn. "Outsider." He shook his head again. "I *wanted* you here. I've been wanting to show you Cedarpoint for weeks. I like to be with you, Alisha. Surely you know that by now."

She swiped at the dark bangs growing damp with perspiration and looked up at him, an appealing gleam in her blue eyes. "Well, you told me once that folks in Appalachia are friendly."

"Yeah . . . real friendly," Zach muttered, covering the distance between them in one fluid motion.

One arm draped across the back of the seat, he tilted Alisha's head upward until she thought she would drown in the smoky pools of his eyes. There was tenderness there. Something else, too. Something a little frightening . . . and infinitely exciting. She refused to close her eyes. The last time she'd closed them while in Zach's arms, he had disappeared.

Her lips were trembling when at last he covered them with his own. Only then did she allow the dark veil of her lashes to flutter shut. Timidly, she lifted her arms and locked them about his neck, surrendering to the rapture of the moment.

When she opened her eyes, Zach was staring at her as if memorizing every feature of her face.

"Should I say, 'I'm sorry?'"

"I hope you aren't," Alisha whispered. "I'm not. Surprised, maybe, but not sorry."

"Surprised? But surely you've been kissed before."

"A few times . . . but nothing like this."

Abruptly, he released her and moved away, his jaw tensing. Leaning on the steering wheel, he gazed out into the road. "I'm not sorry either, but I shouldn't have done it." He turned toward her and held her with his gaze. "There's no future for us, and I don't want you to be hurt. I think too much of you for that. Do you believe me?"

"I believe anything you tell me, but I don't see how one kiss could hurt either of us."

Zach forced a smile and started the car. After weeks of holding his emotions in check, why had he suddenly thrown caution to the winds? When he thought about it, he realized he had behaved much like an alcoholic who has repeatedly shoved temptation aside, only to succumb in a single weak moment.

He wanted to explain, but the hurt and frustration penetrated too deeply, and he couldn't find the words. Somehow he must summon the strength to stay away from her for the rest of the summer.

But the damage had already been done. His caress had stirred Alisha to the depths of her being. What she was feeling now was a tidal wave of emotion.

She recalled Mirian's words: *Once you've been loved by a Martin, no one else will do*. Alisha now knew exactly what she meant.

chapter
9

"YOU MISSED ALL THE EXCITEMENT!" Tammy rushed down the gangplank to greet Zach and Alisha when they caught up with the *Laurel* at the next port.

They looked at each other, mystified.

"Someone ransacked our stateroom last night," she said in explanation.

"What!"

Tammy's eyes sparkled, her red hair flaming in the late-afternoon sun. "It happened during the show. When I left the room, everything was all right. I locked the door and had the key with me. When the show was over, I went upstairs to grab my purse so that I could go uptown with some of the gang. The door had been forced open, and everything turned upside down—even the mattresses!"

"Was anything stolen?" Alisha asked.

"Nothing of mine, but the police want to know if anything of yours is missing. They'll check back in a few hours."

Zach and Alisha hurried up to the stateroom with Tammy leading the way, two steps at a time. "I tried to straighten up a little," she said, shrugging apologetically, "but, well . . . as you can see, it's still a mess. Needless to say, I didn't sleep here last night."

Alisha was appalled. The contents of overturned drawers spilled onto the floor. Clothes had been ripped from their hangers, and the beds were still in disarray.

"Did you have anything of value here?" Zach asked her as they surveyed the wreckage.

"Only my clothes. I have a few pieces of good jewelry, but I keep them in the office safe as Paul told us to." Alisha took a quick inventory of the room, rehanging some of her clothes as she did so and returning personal items to the drawers. Shaking her head, she said, "I don't see anything missing. Tammy, was ours the only stateroom that was disturbed?"

"Yeah. That's the real riddle. Not another thing on this whole boat was touched. Some of the students hadn't even bothered to lock their rooms."

"Well, it's a complete mystery to—" Alisha broke off, her eyes falling on the table beside her bunk. "Where's my book?" She hurried to the bed and looked under it, pushing magazines and newspapers aside.

"What book?" Zach asked.

"You know, the one I told you about ... the one describing the Underground Railroad. Have you seen it, Tammy?"

Tammy, perched on the top bunk, swung her feet rhythmically. "Nope. I don't remember seeing a book before or after the break-in, but I haven't been in here very much."

"But why would anyone want that book?" Alisha mused, turning to Zach with a sigh of disappointment. "And I told your mother I'd loan it to her. She thinks there might be something to that story. Now all my clues are gone."

"Where are the rest of those books you bought?" he asked.

"I left the big Bible at Cedarpoint, and the rest of the books are in the box in the storage room down the hall. Maybe we'd better look there."

A quick search of the storeroom revealed that nothing else had been disturbed. But Alisha couldn't put the incident out of her mind, and after the show, she mentioned her concern to Tammy. "Do you think one of the crew could have done it?"

"Anything's possible, I suppose. But whoever did it, I don't think we have anything to worry about now. Dad put that heavy bolt on the inside of the door, so no one can get in that way. And only a mouse could crawl through that dinky hole in the wall we call a window." She tossed a look of disdain at the porthole.

"I suppose you're right, but I still feel uneasy," Alisha said, applying the final brushstrokes to her hair. "I don't like the idea that someone has been snooping around in my personal belongings."

"It's all over now. I'm feeling better about it already. Let's get some sleep." Tammy flopped over on her stomach and was soon snoring lightly.

But Alisha couldn't settle down, and she shifted restlessly in her bunk. Had someone borrowed her book while she was away, intending to return it as soon as she got back? If not, then who would want it? Or maybe she had taken it to one of the other decks to read in an off moment and left it behind. She'd comb the boat first thing tomorrow.

Finally, the fatigue of the last trying hours and the excitement of the visit to Cedarpoint overtook her, and she yielded to the gentle rocking of the boat.

While Tammy and Alisha sold candy and soft drinks during intermission a few nights later, Alisha suddenly caught sight of the man who had outbidden her for most of the books at the Kentucky auction. His shaggy hair had been cut, and a fledgling growth of beard now covered his face, but there was no mistaking his identity. It was Cedric Sisson.

She might not have made the connection with the break-in, however, had Tammy not said in a stage whisper, "We have one patron who sure must like the show." Nodding toward the man in the fifth row, she said, "This is the second time he's been here this week."

Alisha clutched her arm. "When was the first?"

"A night or two ago, I think."

"Could it have been the night our room was searched?" Her mind was racing, putting together the pieces of the puzzle. "Don't you recognize him? That's the man who tried to buy my books at the auction, the one I pointed out to you in the parking lot of the grocery store."

The lights dimmed, signaling the end of intermission, and Alisha put thoughts of Cedric Sisson from her mind. Mike Price had made it clear that personal problems should never interfere with the show.

But after the last curtain call, Alisha sought Zach out, forgetting for the moment the strange rift that had formed between them after her visit to Cedarpoint. "That man was here tonight."

"Now wait a minute, honey." He chuckled, his sense of humor overriding his reserve. "There were lots of men here tonight. Which one did you have in mind?"

"That blue-eyed man from the auction," Alisha babbled on, not giving Zach a chance to reply. "And Tammy said he was here the night our stateroom was ransacked. Zach, I'm scared. What does he want? When you consider that the auction was in Kentucky, and he's here now, in Ohio . . . then the only logical conclusion is that he must be following the *Laurel*, maybe even following *me*." Her voice rose on a note of hysteria.

"Snap out of it, Alisha." He gave her arm a little jerk and led her to a seat in the bow of the boat. His no-nonsense approach produced the desired effect, and she followed meekly. "Now," he said, once she was settled· comfortably, "there's no need to get worked up. The only melodramas being enacted on this boat are the ones taking place onstage. You've been listening to too many of Ma's wild stories of the past."

"But you'll have to admit that it seems more than a coincidence that he was on the boat the same night my book was taken."

"Maybe," he conceded. "But don't let it upset you. Just keep an eye out, and let me know if you see him again."

But even Zach couldn't explain away the fact that Alisha's book, *Mysteries of the Appalachians,* was found the next morning, lying on a chair on the upper deck of the boat. Alisha couldn't remember having left it there. If the mystery man had taken her book, why had he returned it?

Fearing that more of her books might be stolen, she secreted the box behind some cartons of paper towels and kitchen supplies in the storeroom and tried to dismiss the whole episode.

With the help of Mirian's binoculars, Alisha filled her few idle hours pursuing her search for the tunnel. When she spotted brick houses near the riverbank, she would peer intently at the area for tell-tale signs, jotting notes in a small diary she kept for that purpose.

Although Zach's opinion of the matter was well known, he humored her by pointing out places that could have been likely crossings for the slaves, especially in the smaller towns along the river.

But her quest was curtailed when Mike asked her to be

Jane's permanent understudy. Up to this point, she had only filled in for Jane on the few occasions the couple had spent time away from the *Laurel*. Now, Alisha would be expected to learn all Jane's lines, including those for the lead in the new scene depicting the tragedy of Blennerhassett Island.

When she wasn't busy with routine chores or rehearsals, Alisha spent her time studying her lines and reading anything she could lay her hands on about the island and its inhabitants. The more she read, the more her curiosity grew.

"Paul, tell me more about the Blennerhassetts," she said one night as they settled in Ma's living room for their nightly rap session. "What's so tragic about them?" Since Paul was playing the part of Harman Blennerhassett, maybe he'd discovered something she hadn't yet learned.

Paul leaned back in his mother's favorite recliner and set his coffee cup aside. "Interesting you should ask." He gave her a wry grin. "You may very well be the heroine in tomorrow night's performance if Jane doesn't shake that virus, or whatever she has."

Alisha felt a familiar sensation of fear, but resisted the desire to take the next boat to China. She gulped. "I suppose I should be honored to play the part of Margaret Blennerhassett, but I'll need all the help I can get. Can you tell me anything that hasn't already been covered in rehearsals? Better still, why don't you refresh my memory."

"Well, as you know," Paul began, "Harman Blennerhassett was a wealthy Irishman who came to America in 1797 with his wife Margaret, who also happened to be his niece. They traveled down the Ohio from Pittsburgh in a keelboat and spent the winter in Marietta, Ohio. But they didn't stay there. Blennerhassett's plans included a plantation, and plantations depended upon slave labor. Since Ohio's laws prohibited slavery, he eventually bought part of a large island in the Ohio

River. At that time the Ohio was Virginia-owned territory, so slavery was legal there."

Alisha turned to Zach, who was sitting beside her on the couch. "Zach!" Her excitement was barely concealed, though her words were for his ears alone. "Maybe this is the break I've been looking for! That underground tunnel could be on the island!"

"Could be. Keep looking." He was less than enthusiastic, Alisha thought, but then he had adopted that infuriating air of indifference again. Oh well, she didn't need his help anyway.

Alisha turned her attention again to Paul. "The mansion they built became the social center of the whole area. They called it their 'island paradise,' and so it was until the arrival of Aaron Burr."

"I remember him!" Tammy interjected. "Sorehead vice-president who killed Alexander Hamilton, the Secretary of the Treasury. After that he was so unpopular, he had to leave the East. Where else could he have gone?"

"Where else, indeed?" Paul agreed. "But too bad for the Blennerhassetts that he chose to land on their island. It was Burr who brought tragedy to the family."

"But there was never any evidence of that," Zach commented. "I always believe a man's innocent until he's *proven* guilty."

Paul shrugged his shoulders and accepted another cup of coffee from Ma. "Guilty or not, he went down to ruin and took the Blennerhassetts with him. He was accused of treason after raising an armed expedition, and because Blennerhassett had helped him, they were both arrested."

"What kind of expedition?" Alisha asked.

Paul gave a short laugh. "Ah, there's the question. Nobody knows. Burr probably came west because Hamilton had few friends here. No doubt he schemed to build an empire in southwest America where he could regain his political power."

"I thought he intended to capture New Orleans and set up a separate country, or so we learned in history class," Tammy added.

Paul threw up his hands. "That's the problem. There's no solid proof. But, whatever his reasons, he needed Blennerhassett's money and the island for a base. U.S. officials suspected him, and he was arrested and charged with treason. Of course, Burr was acquitted, and Blennerhassett never came to trial, but the family never returned to this area. Fire gutted their mansion and destroyed many acres of land. Now the whole area is being restored to its original splendor."

"Will we be able to see the house?" Tammy asked.

He smiled at her eagerness. "A tour of the island is on our agenda for tomorrow. We should reach Blennerhassett by mid-morning. That should give us enough time to look around and still make Parkersburg long before show time."

The next morning Alisha and Tammy stood on the top deck of the *Laurel* as they approached Blennerhassett Island. The speck of forest-covered land loomed large and impressive as they cruised nearer, and Paul steered the *Laurel* into the left channel.

"This is the first time I've passed this island in a boat," Tammy said. "It's bigger than I thought."

"I can see why the Blennerhassetts would want to live here," Alisha observed, noting the lush foliage.

"We'll have only about three hours here," Paul warned. "Ma and I plan to stay aboard, but the rest of you are free to roam about."

The waves were licking at the banks as Zach lowered a long gangplank, giving access to the island.

"Like rats deserting a sinking ship," Paul commented as he watched the crew's hasty exodus. "And what do the two of you plan to do?" he asked Alisha and Tammy.

"We want to hike around the island to see if we can find Alisha's tunnel."

When they arrived on the first deck, Zach was waiting for them, a backpack strapped over his shoulders. "Let's go," he said.

"And just who invited you along?" Tammy said in the pert tone she always used with Zach. "We don't need any bossy men to spoil our fun."

Zach merely smiled and waved them ashore.

Alisha had ceased trying to figure him out. Zach Martin was the most frustrating man she'd ever met, but she didn't intend to let his presence ruin a perfectly fine adventure. She caught up with Tammy, preceding Zach across the gangplank.

After studying the map and brochure handed to them by a guide when they left the boat, the trio first looked over the reconstructed mansion.

Situated on the highest spot on the island, the house commanded a magnificent view of the wooded lawn sloping down to the river. According to the guide, the two-story house, originally built in 1800, was sixty feet square, with curving colonnades to the service wings. The room at the end of the south portico had served as the kitchen, and the north portico housed the library, which in Blennerhassett's time had been filled with some of the rarest books to be found in Europe or America.

Leaving the northernmost point of the island, they walked briskly along a lane bordered by a variety of trees, including locusts and walnuts. The path, dappled in sunlight filtering through the leafy canopy, was quietly secluded. Forest creatures went about their business, occasionally scolding the intruders with a series of shrieks, chirps, and chatter. A songbird, ignoring their presence in his sanctuary, warbled from a branch high above their heads.

"I'll bet this is Lover's Lane," Tammy commented. "I've heard that this old carriageway got its name because of an affair between Margaret Blennerhassett and Aaron Burr." Her eyes widened. "Maybe she met him on this very spot."

Zach laughed. "You've been reading too many romances."

"I believe it!" she insisted. "There was a huge sycamore tree where she supposedly left notes for him."

At that moment Alisha spied a building off to their left. "Look! Maybe this is where we'll find the underground tunnel," she said, deliberately changing the subject to one less delicate.

Stumbling along behind the others, Tammy scanned the brochure. "George Neale, Jr. built that brick home in 1832, so it could have been a station on the underground railroad."

Over Zach's protests, Alisha and Tammy jogged across the field toward the Neale House. With a groan, Zach followed suit.

Once a fine structure, the vacant house now looked as if it had not been inhabited for generations. Vandals had destroyed much of the building, and a chain-link fence with a barbed-wire protector surrounded what was left.

Alisha studied the front but detected no North Star or constellation that could have directed the slaves. The side of the building facing the river was missing, however. Nor was there any evidence of a basement, and when she calculated the distance to the river—at least a quarter of a mile—she had to admit that the chances of finding the tunnel here were slim.

Disappointed, Alisha followed the others to the bank of the river, where the three of them sat on the grass to eat the lunch Zach had stashed in the backpack.

The view of the wooded hills across the expanse of rippling water brought a catch to Alisha's throat. The woman who had called this island home must have felt the same peace she was experiencing now . . . or had she? Had Margaret Blennerhassett found her true paradise here—a peaceful haven in which she could see the hand of God orchestrating the beauty of every scene—or, a romantic hideaway for an unfaithful wife and her lover? Perhaps, Alisha thought, the tragedy extended beyond the husband's unpatriotic alliance with Aaron Burr.

Tammy spoke her name twice before Alisha was able to leave the eighteenth century and return to the present. "If you do find that underground art museum, what are you going to do with it?"

"I've been thinking about that," Alisha said. "It should certainly be preserved as a national historic site, but that would take a lot of influence and money—neither of which I possess at the moment," she added ruefully.

Leaning against a tree and munching on a roast beef sandwich, Zach surprised her with his next remark. "You wouldn't have to look very far for help. You find that tunnel, and the Martins will do the rest."

She could scarcely believe her ears! She knew the man was skeptical about the whole thing, yet he had never discouraged her quest. And here he was, offering to underwrite her dream! Unexpected memories of their time together at Cedarpoint flooded her. Even now, Alisha could remember his lips upon hers, and she felt the quiet strength of his arms as if he were enfolding her again. Blushing, she turned away before he could read her thoughts.

Back on the *Laurel* Alisha had difficulty putting Zach out of her mind in order to concentrate on her new role. Jane was too sick to leave her bed, so Alisha had no choice. Tonight, she would play the part of the ill-fated mistress of Blennerhassett Island.

Dressed in Jane's lavish red velvet costume, Alisha did some last-minute study with Tammy's prompting, and when the final curtain fell that night in Parkersburg, the audience reaction told her what she already knew—that she had brought to life the woman behind the story of the Blennerhassett tragedy. *Even my parents would have been proud of me tonight,* she told herself as she exited the stage.

The *Laurel's* journey northward from Parkersburg to Pittsburgh proceeded without delay, and the showboat received rousing welcomes in all the towns where the production was to be presented.

The month of July became increasingly humid, however, and the small stateroom was so hot that Alisha and Tammy found it more and more difficult to sleep. Even with clothes peeled to a modest minimum, their bunks became steam baths, and their dispositions soon reflected the sleepless nights.

In desperation one night, during a stop at Wheeling, West Virginia, Alisha sought relief out on deck. Stripping her sheet from the bed, she eased out the door, careful not to awaken Tammy.

The night was overcast, and with no light from the moon to guide her, she groped along down the corridor. Suddenly, feeling that she wasn't alone, she stopped, peering into the darkness. But when she heard nothing to verify her fears, she moved on.

Fumbling her way to the upper deck, she wrapped the sheet around herself and stretched out on one of the lounge chairs.

A breath of breeze touched her moist face, and she exhaled in pleasure. Slowly, her body relaxed, responding to the gentle throb of the water lifting the *Laurel* on a listless current. She drifted off. . . .

She started awake, straining for whatever sound had disturbed her sleep. On the walkway below, she could hear the unmistakable shuffle of footsteps. Maybe someone else was having trouble sleeping, but it would be best to make sure.

She eased off the lounge and tiptoed to the rail. Stifling her fear of falling into the water, she leaned out to get a better look but saw nothing. Remaining motionless for several minutes, her vigilance was at last rewarded.

A tiny light flickered from one of the stateroom windows. But which one? The light seemed to be coming from farther toward the stern, though she knew Ma's apartment occupied the end of the showboat nearest the *Susie M. Could it be someone in the storeroom?*

My books, was Alisha's first thought. Her second thought was to find Zach, but she didn't know where to locate his berth on the smaller towboat. She crept down the stairs, realizing that she'd left her slippers behind. At Paul's room she tapped lightly on the door.

"Who is it?" Paul demanded.

Alisha didn't answer. She knocked again, softly but insistently. Breathlessly she listened to Paul's progress toward the door, and when he opened it, she slipped quickly inside.

"What . . . !?" Paul began.

"Shhh," she whispered. "And don't turn on a light. It's me, Alisha. I think we have a prowler in the storeroom."

"Get Zach . . . but be quiet about it." The order was swift and direct.

"Where's his room?"

"The one just above the galley. Hurry. I won't start anything until he gets here."

After weeks of crossing the narrow bridge between the showboat and its sister ship, Alisha still hadn't lost her fear of falling into the murky water below. Tonight, however, she bounded across without a second thought.

An emergency light at the stairwell shone brightly on the door labeled, "Pilot's Stateroom," so she rapped softly. She heard Zach's voice almost immediately. "Just a minute."

When the door opened, Zach's eyes popped. "Alisha, what are you doing here this time of night, dressed like that?"

Alisha ignored his question. "Someone's in the storeroom on the *Laurel!* Paul sent me!"

Zach darted into his room without a word and returned wearing jeans and carrying a long shirt that he tossed to Alisha. "Here, put this on. How much do you think a man can stand?" He ran down the stairs ahead of Alisha.

Paul put his finger to his lips, signaling caution, when they met him at the bottom of the steps.

"There's someone in the room all right," he said. "He was stealthy enough getting in, but now it sounds as if he's tearing the whole place apart. Here's the plan. Zach, you stay here by the steps—I can't think of any other way he could leave."

"Could it be someone from the *Laurel?*"

"Whoever it is, we won't let him get away this time," Paul returned. "Alisha, you go to the opposite side of the boat where the college gang sleeps. If anyone comes down the hall and goes into a room, note which one it is. I'm going to flush the guy out."

Alisha took up her assigned post without comment and waited in the deadly silence. It seemed like hours, but it probably wasn't more than five minutes before she heard someone running toward her. Her eyes scanned the darkness to see if the runner would enter one of the staterooms, but the steps continued. When it appeared that the person was going to brush past her, Alisha stepped out of her hiding place and into the path of a bulky figure. Shoved brusquely aside, she fell to her knees in the hall, looking up in time to see him exit to the walkway at the bow of the boat.

She struggled to her feet and rushed toward the open doorway just as the man grabbed the railing and swung down to the deck. "Zach, he's getting away! He jumped the rail!"

Alisha watched the chase taking place as if it were in slow motion. Zach wasn't moving very fast. "Hurry, Zach!" It dawned on her that he was barefoot. The deck must have been damp, for she saw his feet slip once, but he was closing in on the intruder by the time he reached the gangplank.

As soon as the man gained a foothold on the bank, he turned and tipped the gangplank upward. In his haste, Zach didn't see the offensive action. Already halfway across, there was no retreating, and when the gangplank tilted, Zach tumbled into the yawning river.

Alisha cried out in fright. "Paul! Zach's fallen into the water!"

Running to the stairs, she collided with Paul who was coming down the other corridor. Disentangling themselves, they raced to the bow of the boat. Zach was already climbing out, soaking wet.

A commotion from the upper deck drew their attention. "What's going on down there?" It was Mike Price, leaning over the railing.

Paying no attention to the explanation Paul was giving the crew crowding around him, Alisha dropped to her knees beside Zach. His breath was coming in short gasps.

"Are you hurt?" she asked.

"Just my ankle . . . and my pride. To fall in the river when

I've worked on boats for years! I'd better turn in my pilot's license." Shamefaced, he grinned.

"But it wasn't your fault. I saw him tip the gangplank."

Zach shook the water from his hair and painfully got to his feet at Paul's approach.

"Should we report this, Zach, or try to catch the thug ourselves?"

"It would be futile to go uptown now. There might be a hundred people wandering the streets." Zach paused, contemplating. "Didn't we raise the gangplank tonight?"

"I've never known us to forget it before," Paul said as he turned to Mike and the students, who waited eagerly for orders. Someone brought a towel, and Zach dried off, then threw it around his neck. "Go on back to bed, everybody. Zach, let's take a look at the storeroom."

Since she hadn't had a direct order to go to bed, Alisha tagged along with the two men.

"How'd he get by you, Paul?" Zach asked, walking down the hallway.

"He slammed the storeroom door out into my shoulder and knocked me down. He must have heard me coming. By the time I was on my feet again, he was gone."

"My books!" Alisha exclaimed when they reached the storeroom. Boxes had been upended, their contents littering the floor.

"Have you looked through all of these, Alisha?" Paul asked as they stared, dumbfounded, at the mess.

"Not all of them."

"Apparently he'd just found the books," Zach observed as he picked up one book with the covers ripped off.

For over an hour the three of them leafed through the books, page by page. Their careful search netted only a few newspaper clippings, a bookmark, and some dried flowers—nothing more.

"Beats me what that fellow's after!" Paul said at last. "There's nothing here that could possibly be of value to anyone, unless there's a rare book we wouldn't recognize."

"The burglar must undoubtedly be the man we saw at the auction. Did he take anything, Alisha?"

"I don't think so, but just in case he makes another try, maybe we'd better hide these in another place."

"No, leave them here," Paul said. "Now that the man knows where they are, he may be back, and we'll be ready for him."

The hot sun was cracking the eastern horizon when Alisha quietly eased into the stateroom. Tammy's even breathing indicated she'd slept through the whole episode!

Late in the month of July, they reached Pittsburgh, the last stop before retracing their route south. Remembering how much the people in Parkersburg had appreciated the bit of local history the cast had presented—the Blennerhassett story—Mike was directing a mini-drama on the life of Stephen Foster to close the show here.

"Too bad Foster died when he was only thirty-seven. The world lost a great talent much too early," Mike said to Zach.

"Yeah. I know." Alisha couldn't help noting Zach's reply and the accompanying slump of his shoulders.

"Alisha, I've the perfect part for you," Mike said during the first rehearsal. "It's a duet with Zach. You'll sing 'Beautiful Dreamer' as the Fosters—Zach at the piano taking the tenor part, you, on melody. Let's give it a try."

"Should be fun," Zach said with uncharacteristic sarcasm. She couldn't figure him out half the time.

Zach often played Foster's melodies on the calliope, and it

wasn't difficult for him to thump out the music in the traditional barroom manner on the old upright.

Beautiful dreamer, wake unto me,
Starlight and dewdrops are waiting for thee.

Mike was right. Their voices were a harmonious blend, and as the last chord died away, the whole cast burst into applause.

But I can't do it, Alisha thought miserably. *I can't sing that song without letting him and everyone else on the boat know how much I love him.*

Determined to carry on without revealing her heart to anyone, Alisha kept a tight grip on her emotions when she moved to Zach's side during the performance at Pittsburgh. A hush fell over the audience as Zach's fingers heralded the lyrics. As she looked at Zach, darkly handsome in his nineteenth-century costume, with a deep fire slumbering in his eyes, Alisha couldn't control the wild beating of her heart. She tried to forget her love for him as she started the song clear and confidently.

Zach's rich tenor voice joined hers after a few lines.

Beautiful dreamer, queen of my song,
List while I woo thee with soft melody;
Gone are the cares of life's busy throng,
Beautiful dreamer, awake unto me.

Alisha forced herself to keep her eyes on Zach, as Mike had directed, but the intensity of the dark gaze was almost unbearable.

In the pause that followed their routine, Alisha started to take a bow, but the audience burst into applause, shouting, "More! More!" Twice again, with her heart almost breaking, Alisha managed to get through the melancholy words.

When they finished at last and turned toward the crowded room, Zach pulled her into an affectionate embrace and bent over to drop a kiss on her cheek, but her quick turn brought their lips together unexpectedly. Wide-eyed, she stared at him as their lips clung, and his arms tightened possessively.

The audience went wild, but Alisha and Zach ran offstage.

In his dressing room, Zach dropped to his knees. "Oh, God, help me." The embrace that had brought a thrill to the theatergoers had initiated such an emotional searing through Zach's body that he thought his heart would be wrenched from his chest.

Zach had lost himself in the pathos of Alisha's sweet voice, in the beauty of her heavily lashed eyes, the depth of her soul. Her actions tonight had proved her love for him, and he groaned as he comprehended the joy that was his for the claiming. If only he dared!

Rising to change for the grand finale, Zach's prayer transcended audible words. *Lord, am I wrong in my decision not to marry? Would you subject me to such cruel temptation if you didn't intend me to have her? And now that I know she loves me, how can I live without her?*

chapter

10

"THUNDERATION!" Paul pounded his fist on the table. "I might have known our luck was too good to last!" His ruddy face became a shade darker than normal as he pushed back his chair.

Late for breakfast, Zach, shirtless, oil streaks staining his muscular torso, stood talking to Paul.

Alisha came from the kitchen in time to hear him say, "When we tried to start the engines to shove off, there was a dickens of a noise. There'll have to be a delay until we find out what's wrong."

Leaving his breakfast, Paul followed Zach from the room.

Mike was serving up a plate of food to take to Jane, who still hadn't recovered from her virus. "Rehearsal as usual, gang," he announced. "None of us is an engineer, and we'd be better off out of the way." He merely smiled at the groans that accompanied his announcement.

Alisha, feeling the tension of long days of confinement, joined in the collective sigh. The carnival atmosphere of opening night and the first few one-nighters at interesting ports of call along the river was wearing off, and there was a growing sense of tedium. She knew, too, that more than once, Paul and Mike had stepped in before an argument between disgruntled "sailors" could become a full-fledged fight. After one such altercation, a student had been sent home.

At the end of rehearsal, Paul strode into the auditorium, and the harried expression on his face told Alisha that all was not well aboard the *Susie M*. "I don't know whether this is a blessing or a curse," he said wryly, "but the main bearing on the towboat's engine has burned out, and we're going to be stuck here for a few days until we can have it overhauled."

"How does that affect our production schedule?" Mike asked.

Dropping wearily onto the stage, and dangling his feet into the empty orchestra pit, Paul ran his hand through his thinning hair. "For starters, it means we may have to cancel a few performances. And as if that weren't enough, we'll have to travel at a faster clip to make up the distance. Our original scheduling allowed plenty of time for delays at the locks and for bad weather, but now I don't know what to do." He paused reflectively. "Regardless, I won't risk our lives and these boats by heading downriver with faulty equipment."

"What about the show here at Pittsburgh?" Mike broke in. "The theater has been packed out every night."

A slight smile played about Paul's lips. "This may come as an unwelcome shock to most of you, but even though we have only a little more than three weeks left on the tour, I'm giving everyone a few days off while we work on the engine. As of now, you're free. This is Thursday. Leave whenever you wish . . . but be back here by Sunday evening." The dictatorial tone was back, Alisha thought with an odd sense of relief.

It took a few seconds for his words to register, but when they did, the students let out a whoop. They pounded each other on the back, laughed, and danced around the stage in jubilation.

Plans were tossed back and forth. "I'm going home." "It's the beach for me!" "Since we're so near Canada, let's go fishing." "Good thing yesterday was payday!"

Jane, still looking wan from her illness, sat near Alisha and Tammy. "All I want to do is rest," she sighed. Alisha shot her a sympathetic glance. "Hey," Jane said, her face brightening, "we have a cabin in the Allegheny National Forest. Why don't you two come along with us? We haven't had much time for socializing this summer."

Tammy looked hopeful. "But I'd have to see what Dad and Ma have planned."

Mike wore an expression of concern as the students prepared to disembark, and he muttered to Paul, "I wonder if we'll ever get them back." Halting the departing students, he said, "Remember, in order to receive college credit, you've got to complete this tour. So, have a good time, but don't forget the deadline."

Zach, wiping his hands on an oily rag, entered from the dressing room area, but stood quickly aside as the students ran offstage, en masse.

"What was that—a thundering herd of buffalo?"

"I'd say it's the sound of freedom." Paul gave a wry smile. "Tammy—" He motioned to his daughter. "—I'll be staying with the boat, and I hope your mother will join me. It can be a little vacation for us since we haven't been together all summer. You can stay here, or go back to Vandalia to see your sister. Either way is okay by me, but Ma wants to go home—"

"But Paul," Zach interrupted, "the *Susie M.* is my responsibility this summer. You go on home."

Paul stubbornly shook his head. "You know what a worrier I am, Zach. I'd be fit to be tied if I couldn't be on hand to see for myself what's happening. And there's no need for both of us to stay. If you want to go home, here's a good chance. You can take the station wagon, and Ma can travel with you. Roberta will bring our other car when she comes to Pittsburgh."

As the Prices left the room, Jane called out to Alisha, "Let me know what you and Tammy decide."

"Excuse me." It was Zach, looking heartbreakingly handsome despite his oil-stained torso and rumpled hair. "Could I have a few words with you?"

"S—Sure." Wonderingly, she followed him outside to the walkway overlooking the river.

"It's really none of my business," he began, "but Buffalo is only a few hours drive from Pittsburgh. Don't you think you should take this opportunity to go home?"

Her voice was edged with ice. "You're right. It *is* none of your business."

"I've been thinking about you and your parents, Alisha. It just isn't right—your not letting them know where you are, I mean."

"And just when did you appoint yourself my conscience?" She gave him a scathing look. "If you're afraid I'll intrude on your vacation, don't be. Jane has invited me to the mountains."

Zach grabbed her by the shoulders, his hands leaving black stains on her white shirt. "Stop it! You know that wasn't what I meant. If you don't want to go home alone, I'll go with you. We can rent a car and drive up, and if you don't want to stay, we won't, but I think you owe it to your parents to let them know you're all right."

Alisha twisted out of his grasp and held on to the rail as she looked across the river.

"I'm not sure they care," she said bitterly. She turned on him fiercely. "You're judging my family by your own, and I tell you, there's no comparison. I've told you about my sister . . . oh, what's the use! A person like you couldn't possibly understand!"

She wheeled and started rapidly down the walkway, but he caught up with her before her feet touched the first step.

"Well, you can't say I didn't try to do the unselfish thing." At his smile, her heart began to thaw. "I really wanted to spend these days with you, and I do honestly think you should go to Buffalo. But if you choose not to, then come with me."

She tried to pull her arm from his grip. "Thank you, but I've already taken up too much of your time this summer. Just leave me alone."

Standing on the steps above him, her eyes were almost on a level with his. "Alisha, listen to me. I *want* you to go with me to see my grandparents this weekend. Don't you realize that this may be the last chance we'll have to be together? I'm sure after Paul has given us these free days, there won't be any more time off until the season is over."

His words, *our last chance to be together,* penetrated Alisha's stubborn resistance. What if she never saw him again?

She drew a deep breath. "All right. I'll go with you." Even to her ears, the words sounded small and pathetic.

Alisha wished she could be as enthusiastic as Tammy about the unexpected vacation. Her friend threw clothes into a suitcase, jabbering about her two young nephews—who belonged to Zach, too, Alisha recalled.

As she packed, Alisha moped, on the verge of tears. Zach's words had pierced her conscience, threatening to ruin her whole weekend. When Tammy ran down the corridor to consult with her father, Alisha hurriedly tore a sheet of paper from her note pad.

Dear Mother and Father,

Just a line to let you know I'm fine. I have a good job. When I've proven to myself—and to you—that I can be self-sufficient, I'll come home. This is, if you want me.

Alisha

She folded the note without rereading it and inserted it into a plain envelope. Then, she marched determinedly down the hall to the Prices' stateroom and paused only a second before knocking.

Mike opened the door. "I guess I won't be going to the mountains with you, but thanks for the invitation," she said apologetically. "And would you do me a favor? Please mail this letter somewhere along the way. Here's some money for postage."

Mike glanced at the letter without a return address and looked up at Alisha's flushed face. "Sure thing. We'll take care of it for you."

Moments later, she and Tammy settled in the back seat of the station wagon to allow Ma the comfort of the front. Though Alisha had very little to say, Tammy kept up a running monologue as Zach drove south on Interstate 79. It hardly seemed that two months had gone by since Alisha had made the bus trip over this exact route when she had first stumbled onto the little town of Vandalia.

Two short months. The events of these weeks now overshadowed all the rest of her life. She was well on her way to proving she could take care of herself . . . with the Lord's help. She had made some new friends, not the least of whom was Zach. Looking at the back of his head, she longed to smooth the black hair that always appeared to be mussed. She sighed. Falling in love with Zach Martin, confirmed bachelor, was not exactly the smartest thing she had ever done.

Having decided that Tammy should take the station wagon on to Vandalia, Zach and Alisha stopped off at Cedarpoint and watched the two women pull away, with a promise to return for them at three o'clock Sunday afternoon.

"I haven't seen Grandpa and Gran since Christmas, and that's way too long," Zach commented the next day when he helped Alisha into the cab of the blue truck. The pick-up kindled poignant memories of their first meeting.

Zach must have read her thoughts, for he said with a glance at the cloudless August sky, "Don't suppose we'll get caught in another downpour today." He grinned happily at her. Would she ever understand this man?

"The truck does bring back memories—some pleasant, some not so pleasant."

Zach maneuvered the vehicle from the driveway onto a limestone road that paralleled the river. "I'd rather hear about the pleasant ones."

"Well, meeting you was . . . the best thing that could have happened to me, I guess." She dropped her eyes at his quick look of surprise. "I mean, what I've learned from you has changed a lot of things for me. You're really . . . a good person."

"Me? Good?" He chuckled, a rich, warm tone that never failed to soothe the hurting places in her heart. "There's not a good bone in my body. I'm as human as the next guy. Whatever good you may see comes from the One who lives in here." He tapped the area of his heart.

"Well . . . however it works, I'm glad I met you. You've helped me do some growing up." She said nothing more for a few moments, pretending an interest in the various bends and turns of the river road.

At last Zach broke the easy silence. "I'm looking forward to showing you Mom's birthplace. Most of my growing up was done out on the farm where we're going now. As a child, that's where I spent my summers. Come fall, when school started, they could hardly pry me off the place. I guess Grandpa stood in for my own father, whom I can't remember at all."

After traveling along the river for another mile, Zach turned north onto a road wedged in between a creek and the hillside. Alisha noticed quite a few dwellings near the road, several of them mobile homes perched in small clearings. Here, Zach turned onto an even narrower road that wound through the forest. Bushes growing alongside slapped the sides of the truck; more than once Alisha instinctively dodged, fearing she would be hit.

When they had arrived at a place where the creek ran through the road, he stopped and changed gears on the floorboard of the truck. At Alisha's questioning look, he said, "Changing to four-wheel drive."

"You're kidding me, aren't you?"

"Kidding you? Why would I do that?"

"Surely no one lives up here."

"I told you we were going to visit my grandparents, and I'm a man of my word! Did you think I was taking you into the wilderness?"

"How much farther?"

"Another coupla miles."

Deep ruts crisscrossed the road, and at times, they moved across a solid rock bed, so rough that Alisha's stomach quivered in protest. She gripped the dashboard to avoid being tossed off the seat. She sensed Zach's secret amusement at her discomfort and stoically resisted the urge to complain.

"If your grandparents are elderly, shouldn't they be living nearer to town? Surely there would be room for them in that big house at Cedarpoint, and your mother could use their company, I'd think."

"*You* try to tell them that! Mom would be pleased to have them, and it would be less worry to her, but they won't budge. They've lived on this ridge all of their lives, and they'll die here."

"I've never ridden over such a road in my life!" Alisha blurted as Zach braked quickly to miss an animal that whizzed across the road. With a parting flash of a white tail, he disappeared into the woods.

"What was that?"

"One of the compensations for living in the wilds, honey. You won't see a deer like that in civilization. It isn't unusual to see a whole herd of them around the farm this time of year."

They rolled down the windows of the truck and inhaled the tangy pine scent. Tall evergreens overhung the road, the fallen pine needles carpeting their path. Black-eyed Susans grew along the fence row, and blue chicory weed contrasted vividly with the ivory petals of Queen Anne's Lace.

"For years the folks wouldn't have electricity in the house, although the line was near the farm. Finally Mom and I talked them into taking the power, and we bought them an electric stove and refrigerator. Also installed a bathroom. They were indignant at first but finally admitted to enjoying the easier living. Grandpa became a TV fan after we bought them a television set for Christmas two years ago. Gran still isn't too sure that television isn't a tool of the devil, but she watches sometimes."

They swung around a sharp curve, and with a gasp, Alisha's gaze followed the road—straight up! Nonchalantly, Zach gunned the engine of the pick-up, which labored up the steep incline. At the summit, a breathtaking view of the Ohio

River, many miles away, unfolded. Mesmerized, she drank in the beauty of the scene, turning only when Zach stopped the truck in front of an ancient log house.

A shed porch covered the front of the long, low structure, and small dormer windows bisected the front of the second story. A barking beagle, tail wagging, came running to meet them.

"Hi, Mac. Glad to see me?" Zach asked as he jumped from the truck and ruffled the ears of the excited hound. For a moment, Zach seemed to forget Alisha in his rush to greet the elderly couple coming from the house.

"Well now, son, if you're not a sight for sore eyes!" The old man pumped his grandson's hand as if not sure whether to continue or to give up and fling his arms around Zach. The love flowing between them was so real and genuine that Alisha felt her eyes misting.

Alisha's mouth flew open when she noted how much Zach resembled his grandfather. Of course, the older man's hair was sparse and gray, and his full beard was white, but shoulder to shoulder, he stood as lithe and lean as Zach. Gran was a short, dumpy woman and her grayish hair was twisted into a bun on top of her head. She peered at Alisha over wire-rimmed glasses.

Alisha was beginning to feel a little out of place when Zach turned to help her from the truck.

"Say, Gran, I brought a friend with me. Alisha DeFoe, meet the Crawleys. Do you think you can put us up for a coupla nights?"

"O' course, child!" Gran said heartily. "Plenty of food and room for the both of you, but why didn't you let us know you were comin'?"

"We didn't know ourselves until yesterday. Our towboat developed engine trouble, so we have a free weekend.

Couldn't think of anywhere else I'd rather be. I'm going south for our new boat when the *Laurel* docks at Vandalia."

"What are you goin' to do on the boat?" Grandpa asked.

"I don't know yet. Paul thinks he has a good engineer lined up, so I'll probably be the pilot."

"That was a smart move, son—gettin' both your licenses the way you did. Puts me in mind of your pa."

"Bring your things in," Gran said. "I'll get busy and get some supper on the table. Maybe 'Lisha would like to help out while the menfolks dig some potatoes."

Before she knew it, Alisha was aproned and sitting in a big rocking chair on the porch, with a pan of beans in her lap. She tried her best to duplicate Gran's deft movements—first, stringing the beans; then, snapping them into short pieces. But the old woman had spent a lifetime developing that skill, and Alisha wondered how long it would take her to learn.

"I hope Zach and I won't be a bother. We really should have let you know we were coming." Alisha still hadn't gotten the hang of the bean-snapping, and she did want to be useful since they were uninvited guests.

"Now, I'm glad to have you come, 'Lisha," Gran said, dropping the prefix from her name. "Menfolks don't understand a woman's need to gab. Mirian comes once a week, but still I'm always hungry for real woman talk."

Zach and Grandpa returned with a bucket of potatoes, the hound trailing at their heels.

With a sigh, Zach stretched out in a cane-bottomed chair. "Look at that view, Alisha."

She followed his gaze out over the range of hills. The peaks in the distance loomed vivid and green in the sunlight, but the nearer ranges were sun-shadowed as the glowing orb began its descent behind the hills.

"I can see why you like it here, Zach." She inhaled deeply, drawing in the clean, fresh air.

Grandpa sat down on the step, took a knife from his pocket, and began whittling on a stick he picked up from the ground. With vigorous tail-thumping, Mac settled beside him.

"Kinda like it myself—been watchin' this view for over eighty years, and it's purty any season of the year. When my time comes, I hope to be on this porch, lookin' out across the hills. If the Lord takes me from here, don't seem like it'll be quite so far to heaven."

Zach smiled at Alisha and shrugged his shoulders slightly. She realized now why Mirian hadn't been successful in moving her parents to Cedarpoint.

"Reckon we'll have fried chicken," Gran said. She took the pan of beans from Alisha's lap. "Better go wring its neck."

Stunned and hesitant, Alisha rose to offer the old lady whatever help might be needed.

"Better stay here, Alisha," Zach warned. "A headless chicken is a gory sight. Gran will call you when there's something you can do."

Later, when she sat down to the bountiful table and bowed her head for Zach's blessing, Alisha tried to put out of her mind the fact that the crispy, golden-brown entrée had so recently scratched about in the back yard. She sighed. She knew so little about the things that mattered most to Zach— the river, the land, even God.

After supper, Zach followed his grandfather to the barn to help with the livestock, leaving Alisha to clear the dishes away . . . and to answer Gran's forthright questions.

"Are you and Zach aimin' to marry?" Gran asked as she swished the dirty dishes around in a zinc pan swimming in suds made from homemade soap.

"Of course not!" Her cheeks flamed hotly.

"Oh. I s'posed that was all settled when he brought you up here to the farm."

"I don't believe Zach intends to marry at all." Alisha looked at his grandmother, wondering how much the family really knew about this son and heir.

"Oh, pshaw! Of course, he'll get married. He's hot-blooded like all the Martin men."

Embarrassed by such candor, Alisha didn't answer. To cover her confusion, she set about wiping the dish she held in her hand, and Gran put away the leftover food.

"That plate's good and dry by now, child," the old woman pointed out after awhile. "You've been polishin' on it for five minutes. I didn't mean to fret you none. I just thought you and Zach had an understandin', and he'd come to tell us about it."

Alisha shook her head. "No, it's nothing like that. He's been very kind to me this summer. But we're just friends."

"Well, the boy ought to get himself a wife, and if I'm any judge, I think you're the one. It's plain as the nose on your face that he loves you, and if you handle him right, you can have him." She took off her apron and peered at Alisha over her glasses, focusing on the spots of color on each cheek. Alisha could feel them pulsing with heat. "'Pears to me, you've taken a shine to him, too. Well, he may be my grandson, but he's worth havin'.'"

Alisha murmured a polite acknowledgment.

"I'll have to put some sheets and quilts on your beds. Just make yourself to home, child." With that, the little woman bustled up the stairs.

While Gran was busy, Alisha took time to look around. The first floor of the cabin consisted of three rooms. The living room ran the full length of the house. A stone-faced fireplace provided the only heating system in evidence, and Grandpa's gun collection hung over the rough-hewn slab mantel. An ornate walnut pump organ occupied one corner, and Gran had scattered a few tables and some rocking chairs around the room, the design apparently dictated only by need and comfort. By the blanket-covered couch was a woven basket full of yarn. A half-finished afghan lay on the arm of the couch.

On the side of the room nearest the kitchen stood a television with two modern recliner chairs positioned in front of it—Mirian's influence, Alisha surmised.

The downstairs bedroom had been divided to make space for a small bathroom.

When Zach and Grandpa returned from the barn, Alisha pointed to the organ. "I suppose you can play that, too?"

"Sure, nothing to it," Zach said with a laugh. "In fact, this is where I learned to play."

He rolled back the top of the organ, dropped onto the padded stool, and pulled out the stops above the keyboard. Moving his feet in rhythm on the twin pedals to activate the air bellows, he called to his grandfather, who had seated himself in the nearest rocker.

"What do you want to hear?"

"Oh, I reckon they don't come any purtier than 'Amazin' Grace.'"

Alisha leaned against the organ and listened to the two of them sing, again smitten by their likeness. Their rich voices blended in a harmony that transcended the notes themselves, she thought.

Zach's fingers moved across the manual, searching out one old hymn after another, until Gran came into the room.

"See you haven't lost your touch, son." She settled on the couch and picked up her knitting.

Zach swung off the organ seat, joined his grandmother on the couch, and pulled Alisha down beside him.

Soon Grandpa yawned and pulled a watch from the pocket of his overalls. "The time is sure gettin' away from us; it's past bedtime already."

Alisha glanced at her watch; it was only nine o'clock. When she looked at Zach, he lowered his eye in a furtive wink.

"Reach me the Bible, Ma." Grandpa pulled his rocker nearer the couch and handed the Bible to Zach. "Son, would you read the Scriptures for us tonight?"

"Sure," Zach said, and he eagerly turned the pages of the Bible. "I want to read from Second Timothy. When I visit you, I'm reminded of my spiritual roots. The Martins gave me a great deal, and I'm thankful, but the Crawleys taught me about the Lord."

Alisha had never heard his voice more gentle nor beautiful than at this moment, and some of the apostle Paul's words took on new meaning: " 'I thank God, whom I serve from *my* forefathers with pure conscience, that without ceasing I have remembrance of thee in my prayers night and day; . . . When I call to remembrance the unfeigned faith that is in thee, which dwelt first in thy grandmother, . . . for I know whom I have believed, and am persuaded that he is able to keep that which I have committed unto him against that day.' "

Zach closed the Bible, and Grandpa and Gran slipped easily to their knees in a custom of long standing. When Zach joined them beside the couch, Alisha flashed a questioning look at him, but his eyes were closed. Overcome by a compulsion she didn't quite understand, she fell to her knees on the hard oak floor.

Gran prayed aloud first. Then, Zach. Finally, a long silence. *Are they waiting for me to pray?*

Intimidated by the profoundly moving words she had

heard, yet eager to participate in the moment, Alisha murmured a few sincere words of thanks for the day and for the family that had opened their home to her.

Grandpa's strong, sure voice followed her soft, uncertain one, and the Spirit of God seemed to descend upon the room. Alisha knew that here was a man who walked daily with his God, and when he talked with his Creator, he conversed as man to man, but with a reverent respect for One mightier than he.

Here, too, was Zach—fifty years from now. Suddenly the desire to share his life, make a home for him, grow old with him was overwhelming. And in spite of Gran's sturdy declaration earlier, Alisha knew that Zach was slipping through her fingers—just as surely as the summer was running out of days.

chapter
11

A SLIGHT TAPPING ON THE WALL behind her bed awakened Alisha, and she knew Zach must be trying to get her attention. The flimsy wall between the two rooms in the loft had admitted every sound Zach made, and she was painfully aware of his nearness when she went to sleep—at an unreasonably early hour, she recalled. She had heard him turn in bed a few times, and when no further sound drifted to her, she assumed he slept.

The stillness had given her time to reflect over the events of the day, and she had lain for hours, it seemed, drinking in the love and laughter in these walls, the simple fabric that bonded this family so tightly together. An inexplicable yearning filled her before she closed her eyes at last and fell into a deep and peaceful sleep.

The tapping came again, a bit louder and more insistent, and she reached her hand around the old handmade cherry bedstead to return his signal.

"Anyone awake in there?" Zach called, his voice wafting clearly through the wall.

"Yes, Zach. Good morning." She returned his greeting, imagining how he must look just now—his hair tumbled, his eyes drowsy with sleep.

"Take a look out the back window."

She glanced through the small window to the left. The murky light indicated that dawn only now had penetrated the darkness of night. She could see nothing except the tops of the large maples towering above the house.

She slid out of the springy bed into her slippers and drew a robe around her. She went to the window, which had been open all night, and lifted the screen. As she leaned out the small opening, she saw Zach's head appearing at the twin window to her left. He motioned toward the meadow beyond the barn. A small herd of deer grazed at the edge of the forest, and Alisha laughed with delight.

"Right in their own back yard! There are two fawns. Are they twins?"

"I'm sure of it," Zach answered, "for they're staying close to that one doe. I hated to wake you, but I didn't want you to miss them."

"Oh, I'm glad you did. By the way, what time is it?"

"About five o'clock." Zach looked as she had envisioned him. His hair and beard were rumpled, and his muscled arms, leaning on the window ledge, were bare.

As they watched, Grandpa came from the house and walked toward the barn with a bucket in each hand. Alisha could hear the clatter of pots and pans in the kitchen below.

"Aren't they up awfully early?"

"Not for a farm family." Zach's chuckle warmed her. "Grandpa's going to milk the cows, and if I know Gran, we'd better be ready for breakfast by the time he gets back."

Alisha saw little of Zach all morning. Still, the hours flew by. She and Gran cleared away the breakfast things in companionable silence, and when Gran stepped outside to tend to some chores, Alisha wandered around once again. Though the cabin lacked the elegant furnishings found at

153

Cedarpoint, Alisha liked the unpretentious charm of the place—the overstuffed couch bright with ruffled pillows, the ladderback rocker by the hearth. Touching the arm of the chair, she wondered if Gran had sat here, holding the young Zach—crooning lullabies, reading stories, hearing childish prayers.

Entering the kitchen again, she felt that the modern appliances Mirian had insisted upon installing seemed cold and sterile next to the handcrafted trestle table and benches. An old pie safe had been painted a bright green, and the Home Comfort wood-burning stove was still hot from breakfast. Alisha smiled, knowing that Gran still objected to the fine electric stove on the opposite side of the room. She had heard a great deal about the Martin men, but apparently the women of this family had the kind of rugged fortitude required for hard as well as gracious living.

Alisha drew in her breath sharply. So this was a real home, what it felt to be part of a real family. No matter what the future held, she would savor every precious moment left to her in this place.

After lunch Zach had a proposition. "Let's go hiking this afternoon with Grandpa. Put on some walking shoes. I want you to see my childhood haunts."

Alisha ran upstairs to replace her barefoot sandals with a pair of jogging shoes and threw on a pink knit shirt and wrap-around skirt. This was the perfect occasion for a pair of jeans, but she had purposely avoided packing any since Zach had warned, "Gran doesn't approve of women wearing slacks."

They entered the woods behind the barn, following a rambling livestock path, the old man setting a brisk pace through the dense woods. Alisha was glad that Zach did not hurry her. There was so much to see, to feel. Occasionally he pointed out deer tracks in the moist earth, and once he patted an old oak tree lovingly. "Killed my first squirrel in this tree. It was a sight of a thrill for me."

Alisha had noted that, in the presence of his grandparents, Zach often lapsed into the manner of speech characteristic of mountain people of a generation ago. It was an endearing quality, and she smiled to herself.

After Grandpa returned to the house, Zach led her into a clearing commanding an unobstructed view of the Ohio River. Behind the pines stood a rustic log cabin.

"Gran used to bring us here every Sunday noon for a picnic. The summer I graduated from high school, Grandpa helped me build this cabin so I could have my own hideaway." He took a key from his pocket and unlocked the door. "This is where I come when there are important decisions to be made. Here I can shut out the rest of the world and communicate with God better than in any other place in the world."

The single-room cabin boasted only one window, which looked out on the clearing. A crude couch, with quilts and blankets across the back, faced the stone fireplace opposite the door. Nearby, a rick of wood had been readied for winter. Alisha noticed a kerosene cookstove with a few utensils cluttered around it. No luxury here, she thought. Nothing to distract a man from the thinking he had come to do.

"I haven't gotten back here much since I started working on the lakes, but I plan to remedy that." Zach stood, looking out the window, while Alisha sat on the couch, listening to every word. "I haven't shared this place with anyone—not even my mother." He turned and gave her a measured look. "And now you know all there is to know about Zach Martin."

Not quite, Alisha thought. *What makes you so moody? What decisions are you facing? What secret clouds your life?*

"You're the first person I've brought here." His voice was very still, heavy with meaning.

"Why me?" she asked, surprising even herself with her directness.

Zach paced the small room restlessly, and then he stopped abruptly, looking down at her. His eyes were as dark as charcoal. "Because I love you."

She sat, not believing what she was hearing. She opened her mouth to speak.

"Wait," he pleaded, his face contorting with pain. "Let me finish. I didn't mean to let this happen, didn't intend to love any woman . . . then I met you. I know I shouldn't love you, shouldn't have told you." He ran a hand through his hair.

Why not? she moaned silently. *Why can't you love me? Why can't you just hold me and stop all that talking?*

But he was determined to finish what he had started. "When I brought you here to the farm, saw you here . . . I knew I had to tell you . . . if just this once."

Alisha felt her heart pounding uncontrollably. "But why?" she murmured. "Why shouldn't you tell me . . . if you mean it?"

"Oh, I mean it, all right, 'Lisha." His gaze moved beyond her face to the view through the window. "But our time is running short in more ways than one. When the *Laurel* docks at Vandalia in three weeks, you'll go your way, and I'll go mine. It's high time we stop seeing each other . . . before you come to love me as much as I love you."

"It's too late." She smiled at his expression of dismay. "I've loved you since that day I tumbled into your arms when I was running away from my wedding. I didn't know it at first, of course. It took you . . . and your family . . . to teach me the meaning of real love. Loving you has been the key that has unlocked the doors of my life. Don't you see? Why else would I have trusted you, depended on you as I have this summer?"

With a gleaming intensity in his brown eyes, Zach drew her up into his arms. "Why haven't you told me before?" he asked huskily.

Alisha slipped her arms around his neck. "I guess it's because . . . I haven't had much encouragement."

Whatever had bothered Zach, whatever burden he carried, disappeared for the next few moments. He kissed Alisha passionately, hungrily. But even as she responded to him, one small part of her wondered, *What is he hiding from me? Why can't he tell me what's wrong?* She broke away from him and touched his face, tentatively, looking at him with unasked questions in her eyes.

He turned away, and leaned on the window, his shoulders slumped. Silence enveloped them. Finally he returned to her side, and without looking her in the eye, pulled her down on the couch and gathered her gently into the circle of his arms.

"I guess you do, all right," he said calmly, his white even teeth flashing in the dimly lighted room.

"Do what?" Alisha asked, still too bemused to think coherently.

"You do love me." The smile faded. "If it were just my problem, I could handle it."

"Problem? How could love possibly be a problem?"

"Because I can't see any future for us. If we still feel the same way ten years from now—"

"Ten years from now? Why wouldn't we?" Her confusion was growing by the moment.

"Oh, you never can tell," he said lightly. He drew her up and moved toward the door. His arms were firm, his lips tender as he kissed her again. "I've learned one thing at least,"

he continued. "I won't be able to say good-bye in a few weeks
. . . but I'll need some time alone to think this through."

As they entered the barnyard, Alisha saw a couple of dogs,
yelping and straining at their chains. Zach strode toward the
two animals, an action which served only to heighten their
excitement.

He stooped to pet the smaller of the two dogs. "Hi ya,
Bandit. Know it's Saturday night, do ya?"

"What's so important about Saturday night?" Alisha demanded suspiciously, stumbling backward to avoid the other
dog's dusty paws.

"Down, Duke," Zach ordered, and the dog turned from
Alisha to claim his share of Zach's attention.

Alisha's knowledge of dogs was limited to poodles and
terriers, so she looked closely at the two hounds. A bluetick
and a redtick, Zach explained. Bandit, a small, grayish-blue
dog, stood about eighteen inches tall. A profusion of dark
blue spots mottled the smooth hair. Duke, the bigger dog,
was burnished bronze, speckled with dark red. While Bandit
behaved like a petite, fragile female, Duke exhibited the
characteristics of an overgrown teen-aged boy—enthusiastic,
muscular, awkward. He was a handsome animal.

"What's so important about Saturday night?" Alisha repeated.

"Coon hunting! Grandpa always goes coon hunting on
Saturday night."

"And I suppose you're going along?"

"Sure, I always go when I'm here. You won't mind, will
you?"

"No," Alisha returned, not being completely honest. She
had looked forward to spending this last evening with Zach.

But what could she say? So far, he hadn't given her permission to monopolize his life.

Grandpa, coming from the barn with a basket of eggs, barked a sharp order. "Stop it, hounds!" Bandit quieted at once, but a stern swat to the rear was necessary before Duke settled down.

"Duke's still just a young pup," Grandpa apologized for the dog. "Hasn't had all his trainin'."

During supper, Alisha was unusually quiet, and she felt Gran's eyes upon her. While the old lady dished up warm berry cobbler for dessert, she said, "Why don't you take 'Lisha with you? She ain't been on a coon hunt, I betcha."

Zach looked to his grandfather.

"Think you can keep up on the trail?" Grandpa asked slowly.

Alisha shrugged. "I could try . . . that is, if I knew what was expected."

"Nothing much to it," Grandpa said. "We'll just wander around in the woods until the dogs strike a coon's trail, then foller the dogs to the coon." He seemed to be giving the matter consideration. Eyeing her over his spectacles, he said, as if thinking aloud, "Well, it won't hurt none to take 'er, I guess. Ma, have you got some old pants of mine she can wear? The git-up she's wearin' ain't fit for huntin'."

So much for my chaste clothing, Alisha thought.

As Gran whacked off the legs of a pair of Grandpa's old overalls so they wouldn't drag the ground, she whispered conspiratorily, "Been young and in love myself. Knew you wanted to be with 'im. But I warn you. Once those fool dogs get to trailin', you won't see much of 'im. Like as not, they'll forget all about you, so don't git left. 'Twon't be any great entertainment, but it'll be somethin' to remember."

Alisha impulsively hugged Gran, who fastened the suspenders of the overalls over one of Zach's long-sleeved hunting shirts.

"Go along with you," Gran said, but Alisha knew the caress had pleased the old woman.

Zach laughed when he saw Alisha in her ragtag outfit.

"It's all your fault," she retorted. "You were the one who told me not to bring my jeans along."

Dusk hovered peacefully over the old farmstead, bringing the concerted chorus of hundreds of katydids and jar flies. Fluttering lightning bugs lent a carnival atmosphere to the night, while Grandpa fastened a chain to Duke's collar and handed the leash to Zach.

Zach turned to Alisha. "Here, hold the dog a minute, will you? I forgot the big spotlight."

Alisha took the chain, and Duke tugged on the leash until she thought her arm would be pulled from its socket. Then the animal gave a boisterous leap, knocking Alisha off her feet, and Duke bounded joyfully off toward the woods.

Zach returned from the kitchen in time to see her fall, and he helped her to her feet. "I told you to *hold* the dog," he said, and in the dwindling light she saw his teeth gleaming in a wide smile.

"Zach Martin, you did that deliberately! I'm not going."

She jerked her arm from his grasp and bent to dust off her clothes.

"Of course, you're going with us—unless you hurt yourself," he added in concern. He whistled, and Duke ran up, panting excitedly.

Alisha eyed the dog as she said dryly, "I'm all right." One knee stung from the fall, but Alisha didn't mention that. If Grandpa thought she'd injured herself and couldn't keep up with them, he might decide she had to stay at home.

Grandpa led the way into the forest, and straining at their

bonds, the two dogs bounded forward excitedly, their soft paws pattering on the hard ground. Each man handled a dog with one hand and carried a lantern in his other. Alisha kept close at Zach's heels along the narrow trail, but the lights did little to illuminate the path, and she stumbled on the uneven terrain.

Insects swarmed around the dim light shed by the lanterns, and Alisha nervously swiped at them as they whirled around her head. To match the men's long-legged strides, she took two steps to their one, but the blackness and the strange noises compelled her to keep up.

The trail descended into what must have been a hollow, for Grandpa had said, "Let's try to strike trail in Walnut Holler. Always lots of coons in there, seems like."

"Yeah, seems like," Zach agreed.

The ground leveled out, making the trek easier. At the same time Alisha's eyes sharpened, and she looked about her for the gleam of coon eyes.

"Wait up, honey!" Zach called back. "We're going to loose the dogs."

Grandpa bent to unsnap the chain from Bandit, and the dog rustled through the high weeds. Duke tugged impatiently on his chain, making Zach stagger while he fumbled at the dog's collar. Finally, with a clink, Duke broke free and disappeared into the darkness.

"Might as well rest, Alisha. Sometimes it takes awhile."

Grandpa and Zach dropped easily to the ground. When a shrill cry, sounding like a woman in pain, echoed from a nearby hill, Alisha gasped and crowded close to Zach.

"Nothing but a screech owl," he said, and his soft grasp on her fingers calmed Alisha's pulse. "I love to be out on a night like this." He pointed up to a wide expanse of stars, so indistinct that they seemed like a blotch of white paint against the sky. "The Milky Way," he said. One of the stars suddenly shot out of its place and fell in a long streak through the sky.

Zach's grip on her hand tightened. "When I was a kid, I always looked for the shooting star the next day, thinking it had fallen on the farm. Sorta surprised me when I learned in school that the star didn't arrive on earth for a long time, if ever."

Alisha started when he jumped up briskly. "They've struck trail, Grandpa." The two men listened intently as the voices of the hounds filled the night.

Gran was right. They had completely forgotten that Alisha was with them. But Alisha, caught up in the mood of the night, didn't mind. She listened intently, catching the difference in the voices of the two animals. A deep throaty bawl rumbling along the crest of the hill would have to be Duke's, and Bandit's excited yip echoed throughout the hollow.

Alisha jerked Zach's shirttail. "What's going on? Have they treed a coon?"

"Don't know," Grandpa answered. "Could be a cold trail, or might be the coon foolin' the dogs—just hit a tree, run up the tree a ways, then jump to another. If they get after a sow coon with some little'uns, she'll put her babies up a tree and lead the dogs away."

For a long time they listened, then silence gripped the hillside, and Zach said, "Must've gone in a hole."

Eventually the dogs moseyed back sheepishly, as if ashamed they had lost their prey. Grandpa, however, leaned over and patted their heads affectionately.

Again the two dogs wandered away, noses to the ground, wagging tails contorting their bodies. Grandpa and Zach followed close behind the dogs, not speaking.

Alisha jumped when Duke gave a stentorian bellow, and the two dogs vaulted away through the grass. Grandpa and

Zach took off at a run. Alisha hurried after them, brushing aside branches and dodging roots and clumps of earth, running more by instinct than by sight. By the time Zach and Grandpa reached the oak tree where the dogs bayed loudly, Alisha was right on their heels.

Bandit circled the tree, barking fiercely. With a word, Grandpa called the older dog away from the tree and tied her to a shrub. Duke leaped at the tree, whining and yipping, his claws catching the bark. It took both Zach and Grandpa to drag the dog from the tree.

Grandpa muttered, "Still just a young'un, or he'd obey what I say."

While Grandpa tied Duke beside Bandit, Zach pulled a large flashlight from his pocket and swept the beam back and forth into the branches far above their heads.

"There he is, Alisha!"

She spotted two little pinpoints of light beaming from a furry body. "Oh." She turned to Zach, her eyes wide. "The poor thing is terrified—like me when I was cornered into marrying Theodore. What are you going to do with him?"

Zach put his arm around her shoulders. "Why, Alisha, the coon isn't scared. He's probably up there laughing because he's outwitted the dogs again. He knows they can't climb the tree. Duke and Bandit likely chase that same coon every week. The coons would die of boredom if Grandpa didn't come out here to give them some excitement." In view of Alisha's dismay, Zach thought he was justified in suppressing the fact that Grandpa sometimes shot the coon for Gran to cook.

Alisha relaxed in his comforting embrace, following the beam of light. The coon turned away, blinking, and crawled even higher into the tree.

"You mean this is all there is to it?"

"Oh, sometimes Grandpa will free the dogs, and they'll

163

strike trail again, but we're going back to the house now. We have to leave early in the morning."

As they left the hollow, Bandit pranced along like a little lady, but Duke's lust for the hunt hadn't cooled. He strained at his chain, dragging Zach along behind.

Moonbeams drenched their path, and Alisha experienced no trouble walking, but climbing the hill out of the hollow proved no easy task. Her back, legs, and thighs tingled with fatigue when they finally reached the farmstead. Zach took her to the house and kissed her lightly on the forehead before she climbed the steps to her room.

Alisha undressed quickly and tumbled into the soft bed. For a long time she lay listening for sounds from Zach's room. But she heard nothing.

Finally she crawled out of bed and crossed to the window. Zach was heading back into the forest! A beam of light from his flashlight pierced the dark, and she glimpsed the dark shadow of a dog trailing at his heels. *He must be headed for the cabin to sleep. Why didn't he tell me?*

"This is where I come when I have important decisions to make," he had said earlier. She knew that his deliberation tonight would concern her and her place in his future, and the thought disturbed her.

Worried over Zach's obvious fear of marriage and what prompted that fear, Alisha didn't sleep much. She was awake and standing beside the window when Zach crossed the clearing to the house. His shoulders drooped wearily, and his steps lagged. He appeared to be a man who wasn't happy with his decision.

The late-night coon hunt must have caused Grandpa to oversleep, for another hour passed before Alisha heard anyone stirring below. She forced herself to remain in her room, but she couldn't stay in bed. She fidgeted, pacing from one end of the room to the other. When Gran finally called, "Breakfast!" she bolted downstairs.

As soon as they ate breakfast, Zach and Alisha started for Cedarpoint in time to go to church with Mirian. Zach's aloofness settled over them like a chilling cloud. Nothing in his attitude reflected the man who only yesterday had told her so passionately that he loved her. She sensed that if Zach had reached a decision about *them*, it wasn't the answer she wanted. So Alisha asked no questions. They carried on a polite and stilted conversation, as though they were strangers, as if yesterday's scenario in the cabin had never taken place.

During the drive with Mirian to church, Alisha tried to put her finger on the difference in Zach. He was talkative now, more so in the presence of his mother than when they had been alone. As she sat in the back seat of Mirian's red Olds and listened to mother and son, she came to a conclusion. *I'm not coming up here again. I've worn out my welcome.*

At the small frame church where she had worshiped once before, Alisha hoped she might lose herself in the service and forget her frustrations about Zach. But something hampered her communication with God. She couldn't sense the presence of the Spirit as she had when she'd knelt with Zach and his grandparents two nights ago.

When the pastor asked Zach to play the piano, she didn't join in the congregational songs, content to watch Zach, his head bent over the keyboard and his body swaying slightly to the music.

Nor did the sermon by the young pastor bring any comfort to Alisha. He took his text from Matthew: " 'Therefore, if you are offering your gift at the altar and there remember your brother has something against you, leave your gift there in front of the altar. First go and be reconciled to your brother; then come and offer your gift.' "

165

The theme of the sermon troubled Alisha. "If one is at odds with another—a parent, a friend, a neighbor—" he said repeatedly, "God isn't pleased."

Well, I'm not at odds with anyone, so why am I so miserable?

Instantly, there was an inner prompting. *Alisha, that's not true. You've resented your parents.* For the first time, the idea crossed her mind that *she* might have been at fault. Had jealousy of Carol prevented her from accepting her parents' love?

She remembered the night a few weeks ago in the bedroom at Cedarpoint when she had experienced the full flow of the Spirit into her heart. Every time she thought she'd gained the peace with God that the Martins and Crawleys possessed, a moment like this brought her up short.

Was a reconciliation with her parents necessary before she could start growing in her Christian faith? Suddenly, Alisha wanted to hear from her parents—wanted to know what they were doing. But how? She wasn't ready to go home yet. Then, too, maybe they weren't ready to receive her.

Maybe Holly would know how they were feeling about things. She ticked off the weeks in her mind. Holly should be back from Europe by now, and her friend could be trusted to keep Alisha's secret. Now that she'd thought about it, Alisha could hardly wait until she returned to the *Laurel* to write to Holly. Maybe they could arrange to meet somewhere, catch up on their summer activities.

Alisha forced her thoughts back to the conclusion of the sermon.

"Our failure to forgive others often prevents us from receiving God's full forgiveness," the minister said. "Are you strong enough to say 'I forgive you' to someone who has wronged *you*?"

She trailed Zach and Mirian out of the church after the service, convinced that her work was cut out for her.

Mirian may have suspected the estrangement between Alisha and Zach, for Alisha watched her glance from one to the other during dinner. Alisha tried to forget that she might never sit at this table again.

While they were eating dessert, Mirian said, "Oh, by the way, Alisha, let me return the book you brought. I read it while you and Zach were at Grandpa's. The story about the tunnel is fascinating. Before you come again, I'll ask our neighbors if they have any clues."

Promptly at three, there was the honk of a horn, and Zach and Alisha carried their luggage out to the Blairs' station wagon, which had pulled up out front. With a heavy heart, Alisha hugged Mirian, promising to return soon. Zach might not want her, but Alisha believed that she would always have a warm welcome from Mirian.

There was no need for concern about conversation on the return trip, for Tammy bubbled with news of the visit with her sister.

"And here are some Polaroid pictures of the boys," she said, handing the photos over the front seat to Zach. "Unfortunately, that one on the right continues to look like you." Even Alisha could see the resemblance. "Too bad they both don't look like the Blairs," Tammy added mischievously.

Alisha allowed most of Tammy's chatter to pass unheeded. Trying to get her mind off Zach, she stared out the window. They passed several small towns, and Alisha tried to spot buildings along the river that could possibly be the site of the underground art tunnel. With only a few weeks left, she feared that her dream of finding the tunnel wouldn't materialize. She would no longer see Zach, so what would she have to show for her summer except a broken heart and blasted dreams? *No tunnel, no love, no job.* Wallowing in self-pity, she jumped when Tammy tapped her on the shoulder.

"I almost forgot. I stopped in the library at home, and Mrs. Foster asked me to give you this letter."

Alisha eagerly tore open the envelope. "Let's hope it's good news. I was sitting here wondering what I would do at the end of the season."

"So *that* accounts for the pained expression on your face. You looked as if you'd lost your last best friend." Tammy laughed. "What does she say?"

Alisha scanned the letter. "I have the job! I start September 15. That gives me only two weeks after the tour to find an apartment."

"You won't need an apartment," Tammy insisted. "I'll be going away to school this winter—you can stay in my room. Mother won't mind."

Alisha shook her head. "I won't do any such thing. I need to be independent. With the salary Mrs. Foster mentioned, I can afford a small apartment, I'm sure."

Ma Blair turned around. "I thought I'd need to look for an apartment, too, but the town of Vandalia won't have any funds to operate the boat until after the first of the year. The mayor asked me to keep my rooms on the *Laurel* until after Christmas. Don't see any reason why you can't live there, too, and take your meals with me. I'd like the company, and that'd give you time to see how you manage on your salary before renting an apartment."

Whew! At least one piece of her future had fallen into place, though Alisha took note of Zach's continued silence as he tended strictly to his driving.

By nine o'clock they arrived at the landing in Pittsburgh. Tammy clattered up the gangplank. "I'll bet half of the college students won't show up at all, and boy, will Dad and Mike be mad!"

But Tammy was wrong. Everyone had returned except Mike and Jane who came driving up within the hour. The college students didn't look as if they'd had much rest, but they seemed exuberant and eager to go on with the show.

Paul called a short meeting before bedtime. "The main bearing has been replaced, and the *Susie M.* runs fine now. The *Roberta* is heading south tomorrow, too, and I've told the pilot to keep in close touch with us in case we do have any trouble. We'll leave here by ten o'clock in the morning. Tammy, you and Alisha will need to go grocery shopping early because provisions are low. Mike, what about rehearsal?"

"Eight o'clock," he said.

The students groaned, and as soon as the meeting ended, everyone sought their staterooms. Long before midnight, silence settled over the *Laurel*.

Alisha's last thought was of Zach. He certainly didn't act like a man in love. He had even suggested waiting a few years to see if they still felt the same way. *What does time have to do with it?* she wondered. She wanted him *now*.

chapter
12

FOR SEVERAL DAYS THE *LAUREL* journeyed downstream, unhindered. Paul made up the time they'd lost by scheduling one-night stands where he had planned to present two shows. Despite the sultry weather, crowds continued to throng the showboat, and Paul rejoiced over the tour's success.

Ten days after leaving Pittsburgh, Zach was steering the boat while Alisha and Tammy sat within talking distance, peeling the potatoes Ma wanted for supper. They had brought the vegetables to the top of the boat, hoping to catch a cooling breeze off the river.

Paul came swiftly up the stairs and entered the pilot house. "Zach, have you been listening to the radio?"

"No, why?"

"I flipped on the radio in the office while I was doing those reports and heard there are severe storm warnings in this area. I contacted the Hannibal Locks, and the lockmaster said that the Weather Service has been warning river craft all day. Tornadoes have been sighted west of here, and with this hot, sultry weather we've been having, we may be in for some trouble."

"Any suggestions?"

"The *Roberta* has just cleared the locks, so we can go on

through and then tie up for the night. Those clouds to the west look ominous to me; the storm could be full of wind."

"All right, you're the boss," Zach agreed. "Once through the lock, we can pull into the landing at New Martinsville. Do you want to take over?"

"No, you're in charge. I need to have a conference with Mike and the others."

"What do you make of that?" Alisha asked Tammy.

"Probably won't amount to anything," Tammy said, wrinkling her nose. "Dad's excitable."

Paul heard her comment as he left the pilot house. "Who made you a weather prophet, young lady? You two hurry downstairs and help Ma secure everything. I'm not worried about the *Susie M.*, but the hull under this old showboat can't stand much twisting and turning."

By the time they pulled into New Martinsville, the wind had picked up perceptibly. Ma prepared a light meal while they hurried to store the food before the storm struck.

The men tied the two boats securely to the trees along the banks as the wind rose, stirring up whitecaps on the water like frosting on a birthday cake. Alisha shuddered. This was anything but a party. The waves buffeting the *Laurel* reminded her of another storm. The thought unnerved her, especially now, and Alisha tried to force it from her mind as she hurried up the steps to the safety of her stateroom.

Following Paul's orders that everyone should go inside, Tammy had arrived ahead of her. The younger woman stood at the open window and watched the black clouds swallow the sky. Alisha huddled on the bed, shivering. She could feel the boat tugging at its moorings, and Tammy had to grip the window to keep her balance.

"The clouds are rolling like crazy!" Tammy called, her voice high and tense. "There must be a mighty big wind out there.

171

It's bending the trees double on the other side of the river. Uh–oh! One of them uprooted and tumbled into the river. And look at those small boats . . . they're jumping up and down like a fisherman's bobber! You oughtta see this, Alisha!" Tammy cried out. "One of them just turned over . . . and I saw someone fall into the water!"

Alisha covered her ears, shut her eyes, and tried to keep calm, but she couldn't shut out Tammy's nervous chatter.

"You can see blowing rain now . . . the wind is driving it in sheets, like a wall coming toward us. Wow!" she said as the onslaught of rain struck the *Laurel* and splattered her face. She battled with the window, staggering as she tried to keep her grip.

"Help!" she called. "Help me, Alisha! I can't close the window . . . the wind's too strong!"

Alisha stumbled across the room and together they tugged. "Ugh!" they both grunted as the porthole slammed shut. They fell back on the lower bunk, wet and breathless. Then they heard the sound of glass breaking overhead.

Tammy sat up straight, her eyes panicky. "There goes the pilot house!"

They heard pounding at the door, then Paul shouting, "Get downstairs! It's not safe here!"

Alisha and Tammy pulled open their door and groped their way down the steps, clutching the railings for support. Rain lashed at their half-closed eyes and wind shoved against them—pushing, pulling. Pools of water made each step treacherous. The storm surrounded them now, the lightning followed closely by deafening claps of thunder.

Alisha had almost reached the bottom of the stairs when the sheer force of the wind made the *Laurel* buck like a stallion, throwing Alisha down the steps and into the railing. As she pulled herself up, clutching the railing, the hull twisted sharply and plunged down. The rail under her hands snapped. The boat lurched again.

"Zach!" she screamed, her arms raking at the air. A gust of wind caught her, grabbed her bodily and threw her over.

Water closed over her head. Kicking with terror, she surfaced, only to have a wave slap her against the boat. "Help!" The waves threatened to suck her under, and she fought it as if it were a live thing, her fingers scrabbling at the slick hull.

"Alisha!" Tammy cried. "Hold on!"

Alisha thrashed at the water, her legs heavy and dragging, her arms weakening. "The ring! Alisha, swim for the ring!" She surfaced long enough to see a white preserver bobbing a few feet away. She levered her body around, placed her feet against the side of the boat, and shoved as hard as she could, propelling her body over to the preserver. Another lunge, and she was clutching the ring, tipping it over her head. She had it firmly under her armpits when she felt herself being pulled toward the dock.

She grabbed an outstretched hand—Mike's? Paul's?—and was dragged from the river. Collapsing on the dock, the ring still around her, she sobbed, heedless of the touches and voices of the people around her. Then Zach came, pulled the ring off, and gathered her close to him.

"Zach," she cried. "Zach, it's never going to get me. . . . Just my sister, Zach, just my sister . . ."

"Shh. Shh. You're all right now, honey." He cradled her in his arms, rocking her, wiping water and mud from her face.

When her tears didn't stop, Zach let the women take over. Jane and Tammy led Alisha upstairs, holding her up with their arms around her waist and shielding her from the rain that continued to fall in torrents. They took her to the bathroom and helped her to bathe and dress in dry clothing.

All this time she didn't speak. Her breath came in gasping sobs, and she burped repeatedly from all the water she'd swallowed. Still holding her closely, they led her to bed. Jane hurried to her room and returned with a heating pad, which she placed in the bunk beside Alisha. By that time she had stopped crying.

"There, that should stop some of the trembling," Jane said, pulling her close into a long, strengthening hug. "Are you going to be all right?" Alisha nodded, pulling away. "Okay." Jane hugged her again briefly, then let her go. "You stay right here, all right? I'll let the others know you're fine."

After Jane left, Tammy sat on the lower bunk for a long time, holding Alisha's hand, but saying nothing.

Finally Alisha murmured, "Go to bed, Tammy. I'll be all right."

"Are you sure?"

Alisha nodded, pulling the blankets more snugly around her. Tammy looked at her for a moment, then turned and climbed up into her bed.

An hour later when Alisha started crying again, Tammy climbed down from her bunk. "I'm going after Zach," she muttered as she tied a robe around her.

"No!" Alisha protested weakly, but Tammy left the room.

Zach hadn't been able to sleep, so he welcomed Tammy's summons. When he entered the room, he could see only a dark huddle of blankets on the bed.

"Alisha honey, it's Zach," he said softly, kneeling beside her bed. She turned to him. Fear still stared from her dark eyes. Slowly her hand crept out from under the blanket. He took it, and she clung to him.

Meanwhile Tammy had silently climbed into the upper bunk. Zach raised his head a little, as if to address both women equally. "The wind's gone down." He held his voice steady, warm. "We didn't have as much damage as we might have. The glass blew out of one side of the pilot house, but we've cleaned that up already and nailed a tarp over it. The roof on the *Susie M.* is crushed slightly where a tree hit it. That railing will have to be repaired, but unless there's some damage to the *Laurel* that we can't see now, we came through in good shape. Even the *Roberta* had very little damage."

"Wonder how far the storm reached?" Tammy asked.

"According to the radio, the worst of it hit south of here. Makes me wonder about Cedarpoint and Vandalia. Paul or I will telephone home tomorrow."

"Will we move out on time in the morning?"

"I suppose so." Although Zach had been talking to Tammy, he was more conscious of Alisha on the bunk beside him. He rubbed at her back with his one free hand, but her body continued to quiver uncontrollably. So he leaned over her, his face close to hers, and cupped her face in his hands.

"Honey." Her eyes softened at the old endearment, and he brushed the hair from her face. "I love you. I want to help you. You know that. But I can't help if you won't confide in me. Obviously there's something more bothering you than that fall in the river. You'll feel better if you talk."

Her shaking head loosened his grip on her face, but he took her chin and pulled it up so she could meet his gaze. For a long moment they stared at each other. Then Alisha's eyes shifted, refocused. Zach knew she was looking in, at her memories.

"When I was twelve years old, my sister and I went sailing with some friends on Lake Erie. A storm blew up . . . much worse than the one tonight. The boat . . . it tipped, and I fell overboard. I could swim, and I had a life jacket, so I wasn't in much danger. My sister . . . she wasn't a good swimmer . . .

but she jumped into the water to save me." Alisha caught her breath, then continued.

"They turned the boat to rescue me, and I climbed on board, safe. But we couldn't find Carol. We didn't know until we finally returned to the beach that her life jacket had snagged on the bottom of the boat. There she was—*dead!* For a long time I couldn't go near the water . . . not until I came aboard the *Laurel.*"

"And after all these years, you've never gotten over that."

"I was never allowed to forget it," Alisha said fiercely. "My parents wished I had drowned instead of Carol, or I thought so then. They reproached me for falling into the water and causing Carol to try to rescue me. I lived with that for years. I know they didn't mean to hurt me, but as the years passed, I developed a guilt complex until I gradually succumbed to all my mother's wishes. In college, I took a psychology course that taught me that I allowed my parents to dominate me in order to win their love. Still, I didn't have the courage to throw off their domination until that day last spring . . . when I met you."

A tide of sympathy flooded over Zach as he thought of the young Alisha yearning for her parents' love. He wanted to gather her into his arms and assure her that she needn't worry, that he'd shield her and love her forever. But he stifled the words when he realized that that was a promise he wasn't sure he could keep. No, only God could guarantee the comfort and security Alisha needed.

Zach quoted a verse from Isaiah, "'Do not fear the reproach of men or be terrrified by their insults.' Honey, you shouldn't feel guilty. Your sister's death was an accident. If your parents blame you, forget it. As long as you trust God, you don't have to worry about what others think about you."

"But I question my relationship with God—I feel a wall between us."

"Have you forgiven your parents for the way they've treated you?"

Alisha shook her head on the pillow and whispered, "No, I suppose not."

"There's no better time than now," Zach said, and he lifted the hand he held and kissed each finger lingeringly.

"I'm going to pray that God will give me the grace to forgive them, and when I'm settled in my new job at the library, I'll write and tell them where I am. If they don't want to forgive me, then I'll have done all I can do."

Zach could hear the relief in Alisha's voice. He leaned closer. "Do you think you can go to sleep now?" Alisha nodded, and Zach lowered his lips to hers.

Her eyes glowed when he pulled away, and she whispered, "Your beard is getting too long again."

He laughed softly. "I know—time for a trim."

He moved away from the bunk. "Do you have an extra pillow, Tammy? I'll bed down here on the floor, in case you need me again, but I think she'll be all right now."

"Thanks for being here tonight," Tammy said. "For once, I was glad to see you." She tossed him a pillow. "There's an extra blanket on the top shelf of the closet. It'll be more comfortable than the floor." As she turned her back on him, she said pertly, "And don't start snoring, or we'll kick you out."

When he extinguished the light, Zach reached for Alisha's hand. She went to sleep, her small hand in his.

The sun was shining, and the river calm the next morning, when, with calliope bursting forth, the *Laurel* pulled away from New Martinsville. But all along the river, they could see evidence of the damaging storm. While the boat passed through Willow Island Locks and Dam, Zach hurried up to the office and telephoned Mirian. Alisha was standing beside the pilot house when he jumped aboard just as the *Laurel* headed downstream, out of the lock chamber.

"The news isn't good," he said. "Vandalia was hit pretty hard. None of your houses were hurt, Paul, nor was the business district. But Mom said we have a lot of wind damage at Cedarpoint. One of the oak trees in the cemetery was uprooted, as were two of the big cedars on the point. The tobacco barn blew down, too. She says the pole structure looks like a bunch of matchsticks heaped around the old brick house. When we get nearer to Vandalia, I'll leave the boat for a few hours to check on the damage."

"Sure, go ahead," Paul agreed. "You can leave in the morning and be back before showtime."

Although Alisha had thought she might not return to Cedarpoint, at Zach's insistence she was sitting beside him in the station wagon when he left the *Laurel*. Paul, too, had encouraged the trip, probably realizing that she needed some time to recover from her harrowing experience.

Zach reached for her hand when they pulled away from the river. "Are you feeling better now?"

"Much better now that I've forgiven my folks. And it may be that I've overreacted to what they've done. I've written to my friend, Holly Jameson, asking her to let me know about my parents. I told her to mail an answer to Vandalia. I still don't know that I want to go home, but it's a relief not to feel the bitterness anymore."

They arrived at Cedarpoint two hours later. As soon as they pulled into the drive, Mirian ran down the broad circular steps to greet them.

"I'm fine," she assured them, when they inquired anxiously. "But the collapse of the barn has caused some problems. It's time to cut tobacco, and no place to hang it. The men have almost finished removing the old logs, and we'll start rebuilding as soon as possible. Since you're here, let's go down to the site. By the way," she added as they stepped into Zach's pick-up, "I've had a telephone call from New Orleans. The new boat is finished, and the contractor wants to know what name we want on it. Think about it, and let me know in a few days."

The brick structure looked small now that the pole barn had been removed from around it.

"Did you say your great great-grandfather lived here, Zach?" Alisha asked as they approached the story-and-a-half building that was now roofless.

"Yes, before the Civil War. After the Martins built our present home, they used this as a barn."

While Mirian and Zach looked over the area and discussed plans for a new building with the workmen, Alisha walked around the structure. The window facings, still intact, framed gaping holes—the glass had long since been removed. A lone shutter, hanging by one hinge, flapped in the strong wind that swept across the valley. A whirling gust shook the shutter, severed the rusty hinge that held it in place, and hurled it to the ground. Alisha jumped back to prevent it from hitting her and in the next instant looked up at the place where the shutter had hung.

"Zach!" she screamed, and he turned quickly toward her. "What's the matter?"

"Look!" she said excitedly, pointing to the imprint of a star on the side of the house that had been covered for a century by the shutter now lying at her feet.

The five-pointed star, imprinted in stone, stood out vividly

179

in the sunlight. Below it, the dim outline of a dipper pointed in a northerly direction.

"Your underground tunnel!" Zach whispered in wonder. "Mom, look!" he called, but Mirian had come at the first outcry.

"It looks like your search has been rewarded, Alisha," she said.

"Is there a basement under this house?" Alisha asked.

"I remember hearing about an old cellar of some kind," Mirian said as she walked to the side of the building nearest the river. "I've never seen it myself; it's been covered with dirt as long as I've lived here." She turned and called to a worker, "Bring that backhoe. Let's start digging."

Alisha could hardly stand the wait while the workers removed stacks of dirt and debris from behind the house. Half-rotted tobacco sticks and baskets, jars, tin cans, and even a nest of blacksnakes emerged from the heap.

"Do you think the tunnel might still be here?" Alisha asked Zach when he returned from the house, where he'd telephoned a message to Paul that they'd be delayed. "You've told me all along that the riverbank was riddled with erosion."

"But this is one of the few places where the banks haven't eroded. Remember, that first day we passed here, I showed you the retaining wall one of my ancestors had built along the curve in the river."

In mid-afternoon Mirian went to the house and returned with sandwiches and coffee. Alisha wouldn't budge from the spot. She sat in the shade of an oak tree and waited until a six-foot-deep hole yawned before them. Zach went down into the hole on a ladder, where he and a worker tapped on the dirt encircling them. Alisha leaned over the wall to watch. The cellar hadn't extended the full length of the house but had been only a storage area under the kitchen.

"This spot sounds different when we tap it," Zach said, returning to one place again and again. He asked for a mattock, and when one was handed to him, Zach dug into the dirt wall. He soon uncovered a wooden door.

"Oh, Zach!" Alisha cried. "That's it! That's it!"

"Bring me that big flashlight from the truck, please, Mom." Zach reached up to lift Alisha down into the cellar with him. "If we do find the tunnel, you should be the first to see it."

The rusty hinges broke, and the door twisted off in Zach's hands as he pulled it toward him. The door did indeed open into a tunnel. Alisha took the large flashlight in her hand and stepped gingerly into the passageway. She flashed the light along the wall.

"This is it, Zach," she breathed, hardly daring to believe her eyes. "We've found the lost art museum."

The art was primitive and smeared in places by dripping water, but as the man had reported in the book she'd found, the pictures told the pathetic story of the fugitive slaves. One scene showed a man stripped to his waist, an overseer lashing his back. A ramshackle slave cabin and a columned brick home contrasted the life of the master with that of his slaves. Alisha shuddered at a scene showing a child being torn from his mother's arms to be sold to a trader.

They located an iron door near the end of the tunnel, and with his ear to the door, Zach thought he could detect lapping water. "This must be below the water level now," he said.

"Just think, if that retaining wall had caved in, all this would have been lost forever," Alisha exclaimed.

Mirian's tour of the tunnel left her breathless, and she said as she emerged from the damp hole, "Now that we've found this, what do we do with it?"

"The first thing is to post a guard here so that no one can tamper with Alisha's find until we get some authorities here to verify its authenticity," Zach said. "And, of course, we'll have to rebuild the tobacco barn somewhere else."

"I'll have some of the men guard the place for a few days, and we'll build a high fence around it immediately."

"Maybe the National Geographic Society would send a reporter!" Alisha ventured.

"That's true," Zach agreed, "and there's a National History Commission, as well as our state historical society. Mom, you handle the details of guarding the tunnel," Zach said. "We'll stop by Vandalia and talk to Mrs. Foster before we go back to the *Laurel*. She'll know the proper contacts."

Despite the delay, they did return to the *Laurel* in time for the show, but so great was Alisha's excitement that she could hardly remember her lines. For the next two days, she felt frivolous and light-hearted, and her excitement grew when at their next stop a bevy of reporters met the showboat. They questioned both Zach and Alisha about the discovery, and a television team from WMOP interviewed them, asking innumerable questions.

A telephone call to Mirian indicated that sightseers had become a problem too, for the news had spread like wildfire. National historical representatives had arrived at Cedarpoint, acclaiming the tunnel the "archeological find of the century." The State Historical Society had already started a move to turn the area into a state park.

"I propose we donate the land to the state," Mirian said as she talked to Zach. "That is, if you don't mind. We could easily give five acres at that spot, since it's on the lower edge of the farm."

"Fine with me, Mom," he said. "But won't there need to be some money for upkeep?"

"Oh, Vandalia is already working on that. The National Society of Historical Sites will give funds for development, but Vandalia has to match them."

When Zach hung up the phone, he hugged Alisha to him. "Well, honey, your perseverance paid off. How does it feel to be famous?"

chapter
13

A CROWD OF ENTHUSIASTIC Vandalians gathered at the landing to welcome the *Laurel* home for the last time. The calliope had never sounded so melodious, Alisha decided as the steam pipes sounded out the strains of "Here Comes the Showboat." Alisha and Tammy hung over the rail beside the pilot house, waving to the townspeople.

Endings were so painful, she thought with a lump lodging in her throat, but one couldn't expect to live forever in a dream world. Only one more performance—the grand finale—a reception afterward, and this lovely season of her life would be over. When she'd arrived in town three months ago, she had been running scared. Today, she faced her future with faith and confidence. Zach had had a lot to do with that, she mused with a wrench of her heart.

Still, even without Zach, she was looking forward to a new chapter in her life. Her job at the library should be interesting. She would also be actively promoting the development of the state park at the tunnel site, and she refused to lose all contact with the Martin family. She had found a friend in Mirian Martin, whether or not her son wished to continue their friendship. Not that Alisha had given him up completely. Only God knew what the future might bring.

The boat nudged the bank with a thud and stirred Alisha out of her reverie. She followed Tammy to the galley to help Ma with their last meal.

A half-hour before showtime, Alisha was standing at the stern of the second deck when she saw a man creeping up the steps at the far end of the boat. She dodged behind a post and watched as the man tiptoed down the corridor, opening and peering into any room that wasn't locked. It was Cedric Sisson!

She froze, her mind racing frantically. What should she do? Calling out would alert him, so she remained silent until he passed their stateroom and quickly ducked into the storeroom. Alisha peered down at the *Susie M.* and saw Zach emerging from the galley. She motioned wildly to catch his attention.

"What do you want?" he called, but she shook her head and put her finger to her lips. Zach must have understood, for he ran nimbly to the deck of the *Laurel.* Alisha met him at the foot of the steps.

"That man is in the storeroom again," she whispered. "And it *is* Cedric Sisson!"

"I'd forgotten all about him."

"Apparently, he hasn't forgotten us. Where's Paul? We may need some help."

Alisha hurriedly summoned Paul and Mike, and the three men quietly took up positions around the storeroom. Zach leaned forward and jerked open the door. They heard a startled gasp, then silence, before a hurtling form burst through the door. The three waiting men closed in, caught the intruder, and hustled him back into the room. Alisha slipped in behind them and closed the door firmly.

"All right, buddy. What's up? Why've you been sacking the *Laurel?*" Paul asked.

Sisson stared at them, his lips tight.

"We don't have time to fool around. Let's just tie him up and call the police," Mike suggested. "No reason to ruin our big night because of this guy."

Paul studied Sisson's face. "Don't I know you? Yeah . . . you're a deckhand on the *Roberta*. No wonder you've been able to keep up with us all summer."

"Whatever you're looking for, we don't have it, buddy," Zach said. "But I'll have to admit, we're curious. Just exactly what *are* you after?"

Sisson appeared to be considering his predicament. "Won't hurt to tell you, I reckon. Two days before the old Sprague woman died," he said, "she drew five thousand dollars out of her banking account. I know, because I was standin' in line behind her when she got the money. That night she took sick and died at the hospital. No way she coulda used that money."

"But what right do *you* have to it?" Zach demanded.

"Might as well be me as anybody. She didn't have no kin."

"She could have spent it for lots of things."

"I don't think so. My cousin works for the lawyer who settled the estate, and he said she didn't take no money to the hospital, and the appraisers didn't find none in the house. I think she hid it someplace."

"Certainly not on the *Laurel!*" Zach said. "All we bought at that auction was a few farm tools and a box of books."

"My cousin and me looked through everything the night before the sale, but we didn't think about them books. I figured she might have put the money between the pages, so I decided to buy 'em and see what I could find. This young lady"—He nodded toward Alisha. "—made it right hard for me. When I couldn't find any money in *my* books, I thought *she* must have it."

"Well, I can assure you there's no money in those books," Zach said. "That last night you were on board . . . and dumped me in the river . . . we went over these books, page by page. There's nothing there."

"It's almost time for the show, folks," Mike reminded them. "Let's call the police and get rid of this guy."

"Oh, let him go," Zach said wearily. "They'd only nail him for breaking and entering. He didn't actually take anything."

"Okay by me," Paul conceded reluctantly. Turning to Sisson, he growled, "But you're fired, mister. You'll never work for us again. Now, get off this boat and don't show your face around here again."

Sisson, escorted by Mike and Paul, scurried out without a backward look.

"Another puzzle solved." Zach smiled down at Alisha. "You'll be leaving the *Laurel* with all your mysteries cleared up."

"Not all of them."

"What else could you possibly be curious about?"

"I wonder what happened to that five thousand."

"You're beyond help." He sighed. "But we'd better forget about mysteries. This is our last night to wow the audience, so let's go."

For the grand finale, Mike had arranged a show that combined the best acts of the summer. Alisha and Tammy opened with their singing-acting version of "Grandfather's Clock," always a crowd-pleaser. A magic act, a juggling act, and several musical numbers followed. The first scene ended with the entire cast, dressed in Gay Nineties costumes, sitting on the deck of a make-believe steamboat and singing "Cruising Down the River."

The main performance of the evening was the best-loved

showboat melodrama of all time, "Ten Nights in a Barroom." The audience booed the evil bar owner who bragged that after ten nights in his barroom, a person would be hooked for life. They applauded the daughter of the town drunk who had lost all of his wealth to the saloon keeper. They cried when the little girl died, cheered again when her father reformed and the saloon keeper changed his ways. The temperance play, acted in the style of the showboat era, might be an anachronism, but the audience received it with wild enthusiasm.

As a final treat, Mike presented the Stephen Foster story, with a full musical offering of Foster's favorites. At rehearsal he'd said, "And, Zach, I want you and Alisha to end the show with 'Beautiful Dreamer.' I want it just like you performed it in Pittsburgh—" He paused and slanted a meaningful glance that included both of them. "And don't leave out that good-by kiss."

"That was just an accident, Mike," Zach protested. "We didn't intend that to happen."

"Then let's have another 'accident.'" Mike grinned. "Our closing-night audience will love it."

Zach was plainly unhappy about it, and while Alisha longed to be in his arms one more time, she loathed the idea of "acting" the part. Nor did she relish having her new neighbors in Vandalia know that she harbored a hopeless love for Zach Martin. If they went through with Mike's plan, the fact would be written all over her face!

But they followed his direction to the letter, giving Mike the kiss and everything else he had asked for. Alisha knew she had never performed so well as when she leaned on the old upright and sang, her heart in her eyes. She and Zach rendered the haunting words to perfection. His kiss was not unexpected this time, and she accepted it without any visible

188

reaction, although her flesh grew warm as he cradled her in his arms.

The curtain dropped momentarily, only to rise again on the assembled cast singing "Beautiful Ohio." The reverberating applause was proof that the production had exceeded expectations.

All smiles, Paul clapped Mike on the shoulder, hugged Alisha and Tammy, and even enveloped Zach in a bear hug. "I guess the Martins and Blairs can still run a showboat, eh, fella?"

At the reception in the River Hotel, Alisha stood at Zach's side, accepting the plaudits of the well-wishers. There were some familiar faces—the waitress in the small café with her terminal case of hero worship, the proprietor of the hotel, Mrs. Foster from the library—and a horde of strangers, all eloquent in their praise of the show.

Alisha felt as though she had shaken at least a hundred hands when she turned to receive the next guest in the long line . . . and stood, staring in disbelief. Zach, seeing her face, turned to regard the couple curiously. He didn't know the people—a short, balding man and his companion, a middle-aged woman with what seemed a perpetual frown on her face.

"Well, Alisha," the woman said in disapproving tones.

"How did you know I was here?" She turned to Zach, her eyes glittering. "Did *you* tell them where I was?"

Taken aback, Zach replied, "I haven't the slightest idea what you're talking about. Is this someone I'm supposed to know?"

"My parents, Alfred and Ethel DeFoe." She inclined her head toward the tall man standing at her side. "Zach Martin." She made the introduction briefly and with savage restraint.

"*No one* was good enough to let us know where you were,

189

Alisha, so don't blame Mr. Martin, who apparently wanted to keep you to himself," Mrs. DeFoe said.

Alisha's face colored, and Zach frowned in confusion.

For the first time, Alisha's father spoke up. "Perhaps you don't know, Alisha, that your discovery of the Underground Railroad Tunnel made the national news. We saw your picture on our local TV station. That was our first clue to your whereabouts."

"Did you see the show tonight?" Alisha asked quickly, searching their faces.

"Yes, we were there," Mrs. DeFoe said. No word of criticism . . . or praise. Nothing.

"Why don't we fill our plates and find a table," Zach said, trying to bridge the awful moment with action.

They selected items from the buffet and seated themselves at a table overlooking the river.

Alisha ventured what she hoped would be a safe topic of conversation. "You'll be pleased to know that I've found a full-time job."

"What kind of job?" her mother demanded. "Not more acting, I hope."

"Mother," Alisha said defensively, "I couldn't have found a better place in the world to be this summer. Paul Blair ran the *Laurel* as if it were a Sunday school. He wouldn't put up with any foolishness at all. It's been . . . the most wonderful experience of my life."

"Yes, so we overheard in the auditorium tonight." Her words were laced with sarcasm.

Zach wondered how much more of their baiting he should endure before he ran interference.

"My job is at the local library," Alisha continued. "I'll be working in the historical research room. So, you see, the education you provided for me won't be wasted."

Zach could sense a complete change in Alisha's personality in the company of her parents—she wasn't herself. Subconsciously, she was still trying to win their approval.

"Then you have no intention of returning home to honor your commitment to Theodore?" her mother said tartly.

Alisha stiffened. "How can you even ask, Mother? Marrying Theodore was not *my* idea."

"Perhaps you have other plans," Mr. DeFoe said, looking pointedly at Zach. "What *are* your intentions toward my daughter, young man? We've seen and heard enough tonight to know that you've besmirched Alisha's reputation with that passionate scene onstage tonight, and this running around all over the country, unchaperoned."

"Father!"

Before Zach could defend himself, Mrs. DeFoe said, "What has come over you, Alisha? We realize that this generation thinks nothing of living together before marriage, and goodness knows what else, but surely we trained *you* better than that. If Carol had . . ."

"Please don't mention Carol's name to me again!" Alisha cried so bitterly that Mrs. DeFoe stared at her in amazement.

Zach struggled to control his anger. "I'm not sure what you're suggesting, but you can be sure I've done nothing to hurt Alisha's reputation. And as for my 'intentions,' I don't *intend* to marry anyone. Alisha has known that from the beginning. I haven't deceived her."

Alisha rose from her chair, her face chalky white. "Why did you have to come, Mother, Father? In these three months I've learned that I don't have to take your domination, your hatred, your insults. I can take care of myself." She turned fiercely on Zach. "And as for you, Zach Martin, I don't need you, either!"

She turned abruptly and ran from the room. Zach stood,

but before he left, he said to the DeFoes, "Now let me tell you something, and you hear me well. Do you know what you've done to Alisha? Ever since your other daughter died, Alisha has felt guilty, unwanted, thinking you wished her dead instead of Carol. This summer, for the first time, she's felt free, loved, fulfilled. She tackled a tough job and did it well. But you haven't had the good grace to give her a single word of encouragement."

"That isn't true!" Mrs. DeFoe protested. "We miss Carol, it's true, but we've given Alisha everything."

"Everything . . . except love," Zach said. "You've spent so much time pining for the lost child that you've ignored the one you still had with you."

The DeFoes stared at him.

"Unfortunately—" Zach closed his eyes for a moment, then opened them and fixed the bewildered couple with a steady gaze. "—I'm no better than you. I love Alisha more than I have any right to, but I can't marry her. Marriage to me would probably bring her more unhappiness than she feels now, and I've hurt her enough already. She's young, and someday, she'll forget all about me and marry someone else. I intend to give her some space to find that someone. I advise you to do the same. Alisha isn't a little girl anymore, in case you hadn't noticed." He paused to allow the significance of his statement to break upon their minds. "She's a woman, a pretty terrific woman."

Zach turned from them and walked away. Trembling inside, he searched the crowd for Mirian. "Let's go home, Mom."

As Zach drove the Olds away from the landing, he gave the old showboat a parting salute. His work on the *Laurel* was done.

chapter
14

CHANGES IN THE FOLIAGE ALONG the riverbank signaled the passing of summer into autumn. When the *Laurel* docked at Vandalia on Labor Day, the leaves were still wearing vivid hues of green, but each week thereafter, Alisha could see the summer dying. Not without a final encore, however. At first the willows turned a pale yellow, then the maple leaves flamed red and orange. Now the beech trees were garmented in brown, while the oaks on the opposite hill clung to their faded green leaves, as if reluctant to part with them.

Alisha helped Ma with the dishes after they'd finished their Sunday lunch. Then she climbed to the upper deck of the *Laurel* and sank down on one of the lounge chairs. She drew Holly's three-page letter from the pocket of her jeans and read it again, taking particular note of the part about her parents.

Your hasty departure from the wedding really created a commotion, Lish. Your mother went into hysterics, and your father rushed her to the emergency room. Everything was chaos. Theodore looked like a crazed animal—his pride, of course. I, for one, was delighted. You know I was never crazy about the idea of your marrying Theo. You deserve a lot better. And now you've found Zach—hope something works out for you there.

But back to your parents. I learned when I returned from Europe that they've been terribly upset about your disappearance. Your father even hired detectives to look for you. I won't tell them where you are, of course, but it might be well if you'd let them know something . . . soon.

The letter had been written a month earlier, and Holly obviously hadn't known anything about the DeFoes' Vandalia visit. Still, she'd said enough in her letter to cause Alisha many fretful hours.

Alisha put the letter in her pocket and picked up a book. She had intended to read for a while, but the pages remained unturned. Exhausted in mind and body, it was easier to sit and do nothing.

Full and interesting days permitted little time for thinking, for which she was grateful. Alisha liked her job at the library, where she worked long hours sorting historical documents. By bedtime she was ready for sleep, only to awaken almost every night when a towboat went by, wondering if it might be Zach. When she allowed herself to admit it, she knew that the new job, finding the tunnel, and her success on the showboat were small compensation for losing Zach.

Try as she would, she couldn't get him off her mind, and she often questioned her decision to stay with Ma on the *Laurel*. Here there were constant reminders of him, and even the prospect of an occasional date with other interesting young men did not prove sufficient to distract her. In fact, the very idea was repulsive.

Her life had changed drastically since September, she mused. Tammy had set out for college in mid-September, with plans to be home for Thanksgiving. Both Paul and Zach had gone to work on the river, and she had seen Mirian Martin once. Only Ma Blair provided a sturdy shoulder to cry on when she felt blue, amd she was her only link to the summer just past.

She moved her lounge chair to a new position out of the sun, and her thoughts rambled on. The preservation of the Underground Railroad Tunnel had proceeded quickly. Mirian deeded the land to the State Historical Society, and on the first of October, the site was dedicated. The Blairs invited Alisha to go with them to the dedication, and for the first time she met Tammy's sister and her two children. A quiet, sad-eyed woman, Alice seemed unable to cope with two active boys, nor did she seem reconciled to the death of her husband.

When they arrived at the tunnel site, Mirian had dashed over to Alisha and given her a hug and a kiss. She remembered closing her eyes, feeling the sting of tears, and drinking in the older woman's fragrant presence. Until that moment, she hadn't realized how much she'd missed Zach's mother.

The area around the tunnel had been enclosed with a high metal fence, and tours were conducted under close supervision. With electric lights chasing away the shadows she'd experienced when she and Zach had first discovered the tunnel, Alisha had scrutinized the artwork more closely. At the far end of the tunnel, researchers had also found some old cots and eating utensils used by the slaves and had been quick to encase them in glass before further deterioration could set in.

Reflecting now on the project, Alisha realized the magnitude of the historical society's problem. The number of visitors tramping through the cavern was increasing at an alarming rate. Though signs were posted and guards stationed at intervals along the walk, there was danger of damage to the crude paintings and perhaps even a cave-in due to vibrations.

On the other hand, if the tunnel were sealed so that no one could view the priceless treasures, what good was the discovery?

"I do wish there was something I could do to help financially," she murmured aloud.

The citizens of Vandalia had not yet raised the needed funds for the project, and Alisha's meager salary at the library left no extras for contributions to the tunnel preservation.

Ma came panting up the stairs and pulled a chair into the shade of the pilot house. "Lands! I believe this sun is hotter than it was in July. I just talked to Paul's wife on the phone," she continued, "and she says the new Blair-Martin towboat will be goin' by this afternoon. She's takin' the kids down to the park to see it, but I decided we'd have a better view from here."

"Zach's boat?" Alisha was quick to ask.

The plump, perspiring woman mopped her brow with an oversized handkerchief and nodded. "Yep. He went to New Orleans to pick 'er up and will pass by on 'er maiden voyage to Pittsburgh."

Torn between an overwhelming desire to see the boat and the dread of facing Zach again, she wrung her hands.

Peering downriver, Ma said, "The boat came through the Gallipolis Locks before noon, so it should be along soon. That may be her now." She pointed to a white dot far down the river, and Alisha stood, poised for flight. "Now, where do you think you're goin'?" the old lady demanded. "You don't want to miss this."

"Downstairs."

"Sit down," Ma ordered brusquely. "You know you'll just go down there and peek out that dinky porthole. Might as well have yourself a good look. Besides, the boat won't be close enough for Zach to bite you." She chuckled.

Alisha felt the heat rising in her cheeks, but obeyed, joining Ma at the rail. She supposed everyone in Vandalia had witnessed her unladylike performance with Zach and her parents. She didn't blame any of the three for not having tried to see her before they left town—especially Zach.

"Yep, that's it, all right," Ma said at a sharp blast of the boat's whistle, announcing its arrival.

Alisha leaned forward as the deck of the *Laurel* began to throb with the pulsation of the powerful diesel engines aboard the other vessel. It drew abreast—a sleek triple-tiered boat, pushing ten chemical barges.

Alisha's eyes darted immediately to the pilot house, and she lifted her hand to her throat when she glimpsed Zach's tall, slender form with his hands on the wheel. Then she gasped. Beneath the company logo, the name *Alisha DeFoe* was spelled out in bold letters. He'd named the boat for her!

Fragments of past conversations rushed through her mind. Images of all the other boats in the fleet—the *Laurel,* the *Roberta Blair,* the *Susie M.* "We usually name our boats for women we love," Zach had explained once.

Ma stood and waved her handkerchief like a banner, but Alisha couldn't move. The boat passed as quickly as it had come, and Alisha watched mutely until it disappeared around a bend in the river.

"Oh, Zach," she whispered and sank down on the lounge, her face buried in her hands.

The chill dampness of evening had settled around Alisha before she roused. Ma Blair was nowhere in sight.

Rushing down the steps, she found Ma preparing to leave the boat. "Is it church time already?" Alisha asked. "I must have dropped off to sleep."

The older woman cast her a knowing look. "I'm going a little early to stop by Paul's house, but I left a snack for you on the table."

Alisha's face felt hot and drawn, so she took a shower and creamed her face before changing her clothes. Inspecting her wardrobe, she realized she would have to do some shopping soon. The cruisewear her mother had selected for the honeymoon would not suffice for colder weather. She chose the warmest clothing in her trousseau—a pair of slacks and a pink cashmere sweater.

In Ma's apartment she found sandwiches and fruit on the kitchen table. She was pouring a glass of milk when a knock sounded at the door.

"Who is it?" Alisha called out, startled. With Ma away, the gangplank would be lowered and the boat vulnerable to anyone who might want to wander aboard. Thinking of Cedric Sisson, she almost panicked.

"I said, who's there?" Her voice was tinged with fear.

A moment passed. "Zach."

Alisha caught her breath, and a surge of relief flooded her. With trembling hand, she opened the door. Zach stood on the threshold—sober-faced and silent.

Without a word, Alisha stepped back and motioned him into Ma's living room. All summer long, this had been the place where they had shared laughter and endless conversation. At the moment, neither of them could think of a thing to say.

"Um." She gestured nervously toward the table. "I'm just getting ready to eat. There's plenty. Would you like a snack?"

"Sure, that'll be fine," Zach answered and followed her into the kitchen.

She poured another glass of milk. He straddled a chair, and

she took her own place at the table. They sat, each waiting for the other to speak.

"I suppose we need to say grace," Alisha fumbled. "Would you, Zach?"

Even in prayer, his voice sounded strained and unnatural. Alisha had trouble swallowing, and Zach, too, picked at the food. After forcing down one sandwich, he shoved back the plate. "I'm not hungry, Alisha."

Back in the living room, with Ma's coffee table safely between them, Alisha dared a smile. "I saw my name on the boat. Thank you."

"I thought you'd be pleased."

"Are you going to be home long?"

"I came ashore on the fuel barge, and I'll stay a few days until the boat comes back from Pittsburgh. . . . Alisha, I have to talk to you. I saw Ma uptown, so I knew you'd be alone." He paused, and Alisha saw a nervous tic in the muscle of his jaw, as though he were trying to hold back a tidal wave of words.

"This past month has been the longest thirty days of my life. When I'm awake, you're constantly in my thoughts. When I'm asleep, I dream about you. I had made up my mind not to see you again, ever . . . but it hasn't been as easy as I thought." He turned to face the view of the river through the window, his fists clenched at his sides.

"Maybe . . . if I left Vandalia—" None of this made any sense. They loved each other, but it was tearing them both apart. Maybe she'd be better off in Buffalo.

"No!" he protested, wheeling around, his tormented eyes pleading with her. "I've told you I love you, and I'll say it again. But it's time I told you why I can't marry you. . . . I had hoped that we could . . . at least . . . be friends. I couldn't take your . . . anger." He choked on the words, and her heart rushed out to him.

"I could never be angry with you, Zach, at least not for long. But I'll admit, my feelings are hurt. I just don't understand—"

Zach drew a breath and launched into his story. "When my brother died, I made up my mind that I'd never marry. You see, as far back as we can trace, the male Martins have all died in their early thirties. I'm almost thirty-three now." He searched her face. "Need I say more?"

Turning his back on her, he crossed the narrow space to stand in front of the window. "Every morning when I wake up, I wonder if it's my last day on earth. I'm not afraid of death, because I know I'll be with my Lord. . . . It's the present that's getting harder to take." Another long pause. "Until you came into my life, I thought bachelorhood was the smartest move for me to make."

Alisha, trying to comprehend, wore a puzzled frown. "You mean . . . the only reason you won't marry me is that you think you're going to die?"

"Isn't that reason enough?" He turned to face her. "You see, I know how difficult it has been for Mom to rear two boys alone and run that farm and the river business, too. And when John died, I saw what happened to Alice. You've met Alice, haven't you?" At Alisha's nod, he continued, "When John married her, she was just like Tammy. Now she's a . . . walking zombie."

"But Zach—" Alisha cried, running around the coffee table to close the distance between them. "—you don't *know* that you're going to die young. You're perfectly healthy."

"So was my brother . . . and my father. No indication at all that they had any heart problem. Then, in a matter of minutes . . . gone."

Alisha was furious. To Zach's astonishment, she paced the room, muttering to herself. At last she stopped and looked him in the eye. "I've heard some silly reasons for staying single, but yours is the most ridiculous yet!"

"Ridiculous?"

"Do you think as much as I love you that I wouldn't mourn your death whether we were married or not?"

"At least you wouldn't have any children to bring up by yourself, and I wouldn't give you a child that would never know his father."

"Why are you so sure you've inherited the weaker traits of the Martins? You're more like Grandpa Crawley than any of the Martins—and just look at him. That day when we were at the farm, he climbed those hills easier than you or I. Why, even your mother says you're exactly like him. If so—" She tested him with a light laugh. "—you may outlive us all!"

"But I have no assurance of that."

"Of course not. *No one* has any assurance of long life. But I've heard you say yourself that the length of a person's life isn't significant . . . only that one lives a full life here on earth and looks forward to eternity in heaven." Alisha knelt beside him and took his arm. "After the fit I threw when my parents wanted me to marry Theodore, I suppose it's ironic that I'm pleading with you to marry me. But my pride is gone. I want to marry you . . . and I don't care if you live only another week or a hundred years!"

"But I care! I care about what would happen to you if you were left a widow. If we could go on being friends for a few more years, I'd feel more confident about asking you to be my wife."

She looked at him with something akin to disappointment, but there was a good part of sympathy and love mixed in. "I can't believe you'd make both of us so unhappy over such a

201

flimsy excuse. Where's the Christian faith you've talked about all summer? Why can't you trust God for the future? Or—" And she turned away. "—maybe you just don't love me enough."

Suddenly Zach towered over Alisha, drew her to her feet, and shook her roughly. "I've heard enough! I thought we could talk this out like two reasonable human beings, but I see I was wrong." He pulled her to him in a crushing embrace. "Don't love you enough, huh?" His voice welled with passion, and Alisha shifted her eyes away, but he turned her head and made her look at him. "Don't love you enough when I can't eat, can't sleep, can't take pleasure in anything? Don't love you when my body burns with a hunger that no one but you can ever satisfy?"

He dropped his lips to hers in a searing caress. She tried to push him away, tried to tell him he was hurting her, but he gave no indication that he had heard her as he unleashed the full force of his yearning in his kiss. Releasing her at last, he took one last look at her and left the room.

Sinking weakly onto the couch, she lifted a hand to her burning cheek. His beard had left its mark.

For a long time Alisha sat in a stupor. Although she was careful to go to bed before Ma returned, she knew she wouldn't sleep much that night. What right had she to attack Zach's faith? Who was she to question his Christian commitment? And she burst into tears when she realized that in her selfish demands, she had acted exactly like her mother, trying to bend Zach's will to hers.

Thinking of Zach in Vandalia—so near and yet so far— made the days seem interminably long. She welcomed a break in the routine a few days later when she reached the library and Mrs. Foster waved a letter at her.

"Mailman left this for you." Alisha's first thought was that Zach might be contacting her through the mail, and she tore into the envelope eagerly. But the note was from her father. He had never written to her before. Her mother had always penned the hasty notes she'd received at college.

Dear Alisha,
    Whether you believe it or not, we have always tried to do what we thought was best for you. Although we miss Carol, we never intended to give you the impression that we loved her more.

Alisha's eyes stung with tears; Zach must have told them how she felt, for no one else knew.

    We wanted you to have all the advantages we lacked when we married. We thought Theodore was the answer. Ethel has admitted that she tried to live her youth through you—giving you all the experiences she'd longed for. Never having known love as a child herself, she didn't know how to show you how much she loved you.
    We do love you, although we have been tardy in telling you so. If you can ever find it in your heart to forgive us, please come home. We want you here to stay, but we'd be satisfied with a visit.

At the bottom, he had scribbled a P.S.:

    We're shipping your winter clothes to you. You'll probably be needing them soon. There was a frost here last night.

Alisha had shed so many tears over Zach in the past few weeks that she could cry no more, but her throat ached.

The package arrived a few days later, and Alisha sat right down to compose a thank-you note to her parents. At the end, she added, "If you don't mind, I'd like to come home for Christmas."

Dropping the envelope into the mailbox, she felt her heart

lift. "For if you forgive men when they sin against you, your heavenly Father will also forgive you."

She walked briskly to the library in the crisp November morning air, her shoulders straight. She felt ten pounds lighter. Though her relationship with her parents wouldn't mend overnight, each of them had taken a first step—a giant step.

chapter
15

THE FOLLOWING WEEK, A MILD Indian summer day beckoned Alisha out onto the streets of Vandalia's residential district. Some geraniums had escaped an early frost, and masses of mums bloomed profusely. Multi-colored leaves littered the sidewalk, and a gentle breeze scattered them around Alisha's feet.

Passing by a funeral home, Alisha stopped abruptly when she recognized Mirian's red Oldsmobile parked in front of the building.

"Zach!" Alisha gasped, and she leaned against a tree to steady herself as the street blurred before her. Since that scene on the *Laurel* when he had told her why he didn't want to marry, Alisha had had repeated nightmares in which he died suddenly. Last night, she'd awakened trembling from such a dream. She shivered with the memory of a casket being lowered into the grave at the family cemetery. The marker read:

Zach Martin
Born 1954
Died 1988

Is he dead? Was the dream a portent? *Surely someone would have told me?*

She shook off her trance-like state and ran up the sidewalk of the century-old frame home that had been converted to a mortuary. Just as Alisha reached the steps, Mirian opened the door and stepped out onto the porch.

"Is it Zach?" Alisha cried, terrified to hear the answer.

Mirian gave her a surprised look. "Zach? What about him?"

"Why are you here?" Alisha demanded. "Is Zach dead?"

"My goodness, dear, what a shock! Of course he isn't!" Mirian gasped, placing a slender hand to her throat. "What gave you such an idea? One of our neighbors passed away, and I came to offer my condolences."

The breath sighed from Alisha's body, and she sank down on the steps, leaning against the porch post to steady her trembling legs. "I'm sorry to have frightened you like that," she said, embarrassed to look Mirian in the eye. "I-I had a dream last night . . . about Zach."

"Well, Zach is very much alive and well." Mirian reached down and drew her gently to her feet. "But he *is* away right now. In fact," Mirian said, putting her arm around Alisha and walking with her toward her car, "I have a marvelous idea. Since I'll be alone for Thanksgiving, how about joining me at Cedarpoint? We'd go to the farm for dinner. Gran told me to give you a special invitation the next time I saw you."

Alisha's mind whirled. The Blairs had invited her to spend the day with them, but she hadn't wanted to intrude, nor did she look forward to spending the holiday alone.

"Thanks so much. I'd love to." This seemed the perfect solution, and there would be no chance of an encounter with Zach.

"Good. Then it's settled. I'll be in town the Wednesday

afternoon before Thanksgiving, and I'll stop by the library for you. When will you need to return?"

"I'll have both Thursday and Friday off, but I'll have to be back to work on Saturday morning. Would that be an imposition?"

"Don't be silly! It will be wonderful having you all to myself for two whole days."

After the first few awkward moments, Alisha fell into the comfortably relaxed routine of a Cedarpoint holiday. She was quietly grateful to Mirian for not mentioning Zach and wondered just how much his mother knew about their present estrangement.

Ida had been given Wednesday off to celebrate with her own family, and Mirian prepared a light meal, which they ate in the kitchen. Sitting in the family room afterward with their chairs pulled near the glowing embers in the fireplace, Alisha looked fondly around the room, feeling pangs of remorse when she saw Zach's face smiling at her from one photograph after another.

"They've stopped work on the historic site for the winter," Mirian interrupted her thoughts, "but the interest continues to mount. You did a wonderful work there, Alisha, having the fortitude to stay with the search when it seemed fruitless. How is the fund-raising going in Vandalia?"

"Not very well, I'm afraid. The city needs several thousand dollars to match the amount promised by the federal government."

Mirian smiled at her with an expression so like Zach's that it pierced her heart. "I'm sure they'll raise the money—" Mirian said, but she paused, listening to the sound of a door scraping open in the kitchen.

"Mom, where are you?"

With a groan, Alisha slumped in her chair. *Zach!* She looked at Mirian, wondering if the impromptu visit might be planned, but Zach's mother seemed just as astonished as she.

Mirian ran to greet him. "Zach! What a surprise. What brings you home?"

"You know I've never missed a Thanksgiving dinner at Gran's, and I didn't plan to start with this one. So . . . I flew to Memphis and rented a car."

Zach followed Mirian into the room and stopped abruptly when he saw Alisha sitting beside the fireplace. His eyes brightened perceptibly, and in spite of their last stormy encounter, he didn't seem to mind her being there.

"I invited Alisha to spend the holiday with me . . . seeing as we were both alone."

"Hello, Alisha."

She murmured a polite "hello," feeling very much like a fifth wheel. She fervently wished she were back on the *Laurel*—any place except here in this room with Zach. For all practical purposes, they were still miles apart.

She lingered near the fire while Mirian and Zach disappeared into the kitchen for a snack. The first thing on her list of necessities was a car. If she had her own transportation, she wouldn't be in this fix right now.

"Why not join us, Alisha?" Mirian called from the kitchen. "You can surely eat another piece of pumpkin pie."

"No thanks. I couldn't hold another bite. Besides, I prefer staying near the fire."

She knew she was acting like a brat, but she felt uncomfortable around Zach after the things she'd said to him. When Zach and Mirian returned from the kitchen, Zach holding a cup of steaming coffee in his hand, Alisha made polite conversation for a few minutes, then rose to leave.

"You two must have a lot of visiting to do. I'm going to bed, if you'll excuse me."

"Sit down, Alisha. You are *not excused*," Mirian said in a tone that brooked no argument. She glanced pointedly from Zach to Alisha. "When my sons reached adulthood, I made it a practice to stay out of their personal affairs, but after seeing the two of you persecuting each other for months, it's time to meddle. *What* is the matter with you?"

Alisha kept her lips sealed. Mirian was *his* mother—let Zach explain his stubbornness to her.

"I want an answer. One, or both of you, is being foolish, and I want to know why."

Zach grinned wryly. "It depends on whose opinion you want. Alisha thinks I'm being stubborn; I think she's being unreasonable."

"All right, Alisha. Let's have your side of the story first."

"It's simple. I love him and want to marry him, but he doesn't want me."

Zach half-rose from his chair, lifting his hand in exasperation. "I thought we settled that the last time I saw you." He turned to his mother. "It isn't that I don't want Alisha. It's just that I'm not going to marry anyone."

"And why not, for goodness sake?"

"I've seen enough Martin men die and leave their wives with young families to rear by themselves. I'm never going to put a woman in that position, especially one I love as much as I love Alisha." The expression on his face was sheer torture.

"Oh, Zach!" Mirian cried, tears filling her eyes. "I had no idea that's what was bothering you."

"Look how Alice has changed. She's lost interest in everything since John died."

"Yes, but Alice is being ridiculous," Mirian responded. "I've been waiting for her mother to take her in hand, and since she hasn't, I'm going to have a talk with Alice myself. One can't mourn forever."

"But you can't deny how hard it was for you!"

"No. I'll admit it was hard. And I do miss him so much." She paused, her eyes roaming to the framed portrait of her husband above the mantel. "But as for you, Zach, you may not have inherited the Martin weakness. You may be like Dad. You'll have to be dropped on the ash-heap to get rid of you!"

"Exactly what I told him," Alisha interjected.

Zach was silent, his head bowed.

"I'll have to agree with Alisha, son. You simply aren't thinking clearly."

"I never thought *you'd* turn against me, Mom," Zach said as he set the coffee cup down with a thud.

Mirian's compassionate eyes studied her son's face. "Listen to me, Zach. Do you think I've ever been sorry that I married your father, even though we had so few years together? Don't you know I'd do it all over again—for a year, a week, a *day*? Do you think I could ever regret having brought you and John into the world?"

"Do you actually mean that if you'd known that Father would live only a few years and leave you with two boys to raise that you would still have said yes?"

"I wouldn't have hesitated for a minute. Zach, why deprive yourselves of happiness? Life is short, at best. Don't waste it. But don't take my word for it. Let's see what the Scriptures say." She reached for her Bible.

"Don't think I haven't searched the Word for an answer! I've read Ephesians 5 so many times I know it by heart. 'Husbands, love your wives, just as Christ loved the church and gave himself up for her.' That's exactly what I'm trying to do, Mom—sacrificing my desires for Alisha's welfare."

"I don't fault your intentions, Zach. It's just that you've taken matters into your own hands. As Christians, we must trust God to direct our daily lives, trust him to chart the future."

Mirian leafed through the Bible. "Here's what I mean in Isaiah 48:17. 'This is what the LORD says—your Redeemer, the Holy One of Israel: "I am the LORD your God, who teaches you what is best for you, who directs you in the way you should go.'"

Zach still looked unconvinced, and Alisha said, "Don't you think *I* should have some say in the matter. I want to share your life—troubles, joys, all of it. You're treating me like a child, not letting me make my own decisions. That's exactly the way my parents have treated me all my life."

Zach's face colored, and he looked down at his hands.

"Alisha's chosen the right word, son. Marriage is sharing—the good times, and the bad. 'There is a time for everything.' Solomon said that, you remember."

"Yeah, I remember." Then Zach's voice took on a bitter tone. "He also said there is 'a time to be born and a time to die.'"

Mirian crossed to where Zach sat with a bowed head. "I want you and Alisha to enjoy the love and happiness I experienced with your father, but I'll say no more now. You have to make the decision yourself. And now, Alisha, it *is* bedtime. My parents will be up before daybreak, looking for us."

Alisha wondered if she could ever go to sleep. She had waited for some response from Zach, some idea that he could now see that his reasons for remaining a bachelor were unreasonable, if noble. But he had gone on to bed with little comment.

After glancing at the illuminated dial of the clock three times, she sat up in bed. *If only I had something to read,* she thought and turned on the light.

She glanced around the room and spotted the old Bible that she'd bought at the Kentucky auction, lying on the lower shelf of the table where she'd placed it months before.

Alisha left the bed to lift the heavy book, handling it with care, partly out of respect for the Bible, and partly because she remembered the damaged back binding. "The binding must weigh as much as the Bible itself," she said aloud as she draped a blanket around her shoulders and started leafing through the book.

The Bible kept sliding toward the edge of the bed while she scanned the many study aids in the front. She paused at the blank family page, recalling the day of the auction—the neglected homestead, the fragments of a life contained on several old tables, the haunting memory of a woman who had been the last of her family line. With a smile she also recalled the man who had tried to bid on her books. What a commotion he had caused! *Greed does terrible things to people,* she mused.

Deep in thought, Alisha lost her grip on the huge Bible, and it fell to the floor. She scrambled off the bed to lift it, groaning when she saw that the back cover had torn from the book.

Upon inspection she saw that the repair would be no problem. She could find all the materials necessary at the library when she got back to Vandalia. She picked up the Bible to place it with her luggage. As she did so, she noticed a scrap of green paper protruding from the back binding.

She gave a little tug . . . and stared, wide-eyed, at the hundred-dollar bill in her hand.

She gathered up the money and Bible cover and ran down

the hall toward Zach's room. "Zach!" she shouted, pounding on the door, "May I come in?" and without waiting for an answer, she opened the door.

In the darkness, Alisha detected a movement in the corner as Zach turned over in bed and flipped on the light. He sat up, his eyes heavy with sleep.

"What's the matter?" he asked, a puzzled look on his face.

"Look what I found! In the old Bible I bought at the auction. I pulled it out of the back cover."

Awake instantly, Zach threw aside the covers and took the binding from her hand. "Do you suppose the money that guy was searching for is in this Bible?"

Mirian appeared in the doorway. "I heard noises. What is it? What's wrong?"

"Come in, come in!" Alisha cried excitedly. "Look what I found in the back of this old Bible." She waved the bill at Mirian.

"The whole back of this Bible has been cut," Zach said, as excited as Alisha. He opened the drawer of his dresser and rustled through its contents. "There should be a knife here somewhere," he said as he retrieved a small penknife. "Shall I cut it open?"

Alisha nodded.

Carefully, Zach cut the glue that held the binding together, and the cover opened, revealing a cavity full of bank notes. On top of the money lay a scrap of paper, and Alisha hung over Zach's shoulder as he read aloud.

"I don't have much time left, and my material possessions are few. I've prepaid my funeral expenses, so when I draw my last breath, I will owe no one anything. You may call me an eccentric old woman, but I want to leave my small savings to someone who has a reverence for God's Word. If you found this, you have my family Bible. Whoever you are, the money is yours. I only ask that you use it for honorable purposes."

The note was signed "Letha Sprague" and dated the previous spring.

"Looks like a windfall, honey," Zach said to Alisha. He counted the money—five thousand dollars. "It's all here."

"So Sisson was right," Alisha said. They laughed together companionably, as if they had never quarreled.

"Wouldn't he be outraged to know we'd found the money? I'd forgotten about leaving the Bible here."

Not so excited as Zach and Alisha, Mirian smothered a yawn. "It's a nice surprise, but I'm sorry you found it at this hour. I don't suppose either one of you will sleep, but let's try. We have to leave for the farm early in the morning."

Zach handed the money to Alisha. "Do you want to keep it where you can peek at it occasionally to be sure it isn't a dream?"

She put up a hand. "No, you hide it someplace. I'll be afraid Sisson is still snooping around."

Elated, Alisha went down the hall toward her room. Finding the money had been fun, but that the find had restored Zach's loving personality brought the greatest joy.

The next morning, as they drove toward the Crawley farm, the three could talk of nothing else but Alisha's amazing discovery.

"I didn't sleep all night wondering what to do with that money. I need a few things—a car, for instance—but I wouldn't feel right if I used the money for something personal." She paused. "Do you think it would be all right if I donated the money to help with the preservation of the

Underground Art Museum? I'd like to think the funds could be used for some perpetual good."

Zach's pride in her showed plainly in his eyes, and Mirian squeezed her hand. "That's very generous of you, Alisha, but don't you think you should keep something for yourself?"

"No, I'd prefer to give it all to the special fund. I thought it all out last night. There *is* one problem, though." She turned wondering eyes on Zach and Mirian. "If *I* donate that much cash to the project, people will be curious as to where the money came from, but if you or Zach will make the donation, no one would think a thing about it."

"It's your money, Alisha, and if you want to handle it that way, we'll take care of it. And as for a car, this pick-up just sits in the garage all the time I'm out on the boat—no reason you can't keep it to drive."

The old homestead looked as welcoming as ever when they drove into the yard. Grandpa had butchered a hog the week before, and Gran had roasted the tenderloin for them. Mirian's contribution of turkey and dressing seemed unnecessary when Alisha noted all that Gran put on the table—sweet potatoes, turnips, hominy, green beans, cole slaw, pickled beets, pickled cucumbers.

"What kind of pie do you want, Zach?" Gran asked. "Mincemeat or cherry?"

"Both," he replied through a mouthful of food.

"That's one way in which he's just like his father!" Mirian joined the round of laughter.

While Alisha helped clear the table and wash dishes, she couldn't help wishing she were a *permanent* part of the family and not just a visitor. But if Zach had changed his mind after his mother's counsel, he had given no indication of it.

In fact, Zach disappeared soon after dinner, and at the

questioning look in Alisha's eyes, Mirian said, "He's gone to the cabin."

The place where he goes to make all his decisions, Alisha thought, suspecting that, once again, the decision concerned her future. Whatever he decided today, she surmised, would be irrevocable. Zach wasn't one to change his mind on a whim.

Alisha fidgeted as Mirian and her parents talked about Thanksgivings past. She noted the passage of time as the old mantel clock struck two o'clock, three o'clock. When the clock sounded four times, Mirian looked at her.

"If I were you, I'd go up to the cabin, Alisha. Zach may want some company by this time."

Alisha needed no urging. She took her coat from the wall rack beside the door and exchanged her light slippers for boots.

"Do you know where the cabin's at, child?" Gran asked.

"Yes. I think I can find it."

Alisha left the barnyard and entered the woods eagerly, but her steps soon slowed. *Will Zach be annoyed with me?* But after all, her future was at stake, too. She should have something to say about it.

She smelled the wood smoke before she came to the cabin. He was still there. Reaching the small clearing, she paused to look toward the Ohio. With the absence of foliage on the trees, the river, in plain view, gleamed like a blue ribbon as it snaked through the valley.

Alisha breathed a prayer as she turned toward the cabin and lifted her hand to knock softly. She held her breath.

"Alisha?"

"Yes."

"The door's unlocked."

Zach stood with his back to the fireplace. Watching him,

216

Alisha carefully closed the door and leaned against it. Even though the cabin was small, the distance between them seemed like a vast gulf.

But Zach's first words were the last she expected to hear. "Are you sure you'll never be sorry, no matter what happens?"

She nodded. "Yes, I'm sure. Everything I ever wanted in this world begins with you."

Zach held out his arms, bridging the gulf in three words. "I love you," and his arms closed around her in a grip that showed she was his—as long as they both should live.

They planned the wedding for the following month, and Alisha rushed off a letter to Holly asking her to again serve as maid of honor. Zach returned to the *Alisha* for two more weeks, but Alisha was so busy with her wedding preparations that the time went swiftly.

Mirian had invited them to live at Cedarpoint, but both Alisha and Zach felt it best to take a small apartment in Vandalia. Someday they would build a home on the farm, but for now, they longed for time alone.

Holly came with Alisha's parents, who arrived two days before the wedding. Alisha rushed to the hotel to meet them.

After greeting her parents, Alisha knocked on Holly's door. They embraced, and Holly asked, "Sure you won't run away from this wedding, too?"

"No way." Alisha laughed. "I've had too much trouble persuading him to marry me."

"Alisha, I'm so happy for you. You can't imagine how miserable you looked last May. Today you're absolutely glowing. I've made up my mind—I'll never marry unless I find what you have."

Alisha held tightly to Holly's hand. "It isn't only Zach that makes me happy. I'm closer to God now, too. I'll tell you

217

about it all tonight if you'll let me share your room. But now I have to go talk to my parents."

The few steps to her parents' door seemed the longest walk Alisha had ever taken. She knocked timidly and entered at her mother's call. Mrs. DeFoe sat, listlessly brushing her hair, and for a few moments, neither of them spoke.

"Father went to try on his tux." Ethel DeFoe made a stab at some small talk, but Alisha was ready for so much more.

She knelt beside her mother. "I'm sorry for all the trouble I've caused you. I haven't been a very dutiful daughter, but I want to be."

Ethel DeFoe attempted an awkward pat, then ran her fingers through Alisha's hair, as if not wanting to break this first contact. "You've caused us very little trouble. Of course, we've been worried about you this summer. . . . If we could have just talked things out, maybe—"

"I'm sorry, too, that I disappointed you about Theodore, but now that I know what it is to love someone, I know I did the right thing."

Mrs. DeFoe laid down her brush and pulled Alisha to the couch beside her. "I'm glad you're marrying Zach."

"You are?" Alisha lifted astonished eyes to her mother, who looked away in embarrassment.

"This is a little difficult to admit after all these years . . . but I didn't love your father when we married. Your marriage to Zach will bring you what I've always wanted for you—happiness."

"Oh, Mother, there's so much I want to tell you!" Alisha's face glowed, reflecting an inner radiance. "Zach and I can love each other so much because we love God more! That kind of love is the key to happiness." At her mother's look of confusion, Alisha rushed on. "But there's all the time in the world to share with you. Right now, I just want you to know how much I love you."

With the suspicion of moisture in her eyes, Ethel DeFoe embraced Alisha with a new warmth, not the stilted clasps of the past. "And we love you, darling."

O Lord, Alisha prayed, *please don't let it be too late to work a miracle in my parents' hearts.*

Holly fitted the veil over Alisha's hair, and Tammy lifted the bouquet from the florist's box. Alisha could hear Zach pounding out the melody of "Here Comes the Bride" on the calliope overhead. She opened the window of their stateroom.

"That guy!" she laughed. "If he doesn't hurry, he'll miss the wedding!"

"No big rush," Tammy said. "It's still ten minutes before the ceremony begins. It's a good thing you decided to be married on the *Laurel*. Not a church in town could have held all the people out there. I believe almost everyone in the county is here."

They heard a tap on the door and her father's voice. "Are you ready, Alisha?"

More than ready. Alisha took one last glance in the mirror, smiling at her reflection.

Her new wedding gown was the only purchase she had allowed herself to make with a part of the money she had found. In place of the overpowering gown her mother had selected for her wedding to Theodore, this one was simply but elegantly tailored to her petite frame.

The lush heavy satin was its own ornamentation. A softly rounded neckline fell to a molded bodice that hugged her waistline before flaring to floor-length and forming a short train. The sleeves were slightly puffed at the shoulder and then encased her arms to the wrist. She was wearing a pearl

219

and diamond necklace and earrings that belonged to Mirian and, on her head, a confection of tulle that crowned her dark hair "like a halo," Tammy insisted. She hoped Zach would be pleased.

As she met her father in the hallway, he bent and kissed her cheek. "You look lovely, Alisha—the dearest daughter a father could have." He assumed a stern stance. "And if that young man doesn't know what a jewel he's getting, remember you always have a home in Buffalo." He cleared his throat, as if he'd already said too much.

"Oh, Father, there's no danger of that. My world is waiting for me in there."

They stepped to the back of the theater which had been transformed into a wedding bower. Someone—probably Mike, Alisha surmised—had lowered one of the stage backdrops in back of the improvised altar at the front. She recognized the scene—a dense forest on the wide banks of the Ohio. Her eyes misted over until she could barely make out the details . . . or the features of the tall bearded man who approached the altar at that moment and turned a dazzling smile in her direction.

There were no regrets today. No fear. No doubts. Only an overwhelming desire to hurry to his side and stay there for the rest of her life.

On her way to the altar, she spotted Gran and Grandpa, plainly uncomfortable in their Sunday-go-to-meeting finery, seated beside Mirian. Gran gave Alisha a sly wink, and she floated on toward the front where Holly and Paul . . . and Zach were waiting for her.

"Dearly beloved, we are gathered together here in the sight of God, and in the presence of these witnesses," the young minister from Mirian's church began, and the ceremony moved along in the traditional manner.

Once, Alisha glanced over at Zach. His somber expression frightened her. *Is he sorry he's marrying me? Was I wrong to insist?*

When the minister asked, "Who gives this woman in marriage to this man?" Alisha smiled fondly at her father and kissed him when he said, "Her mother and I."

When her father sat down, Zach drew her close, smiling at her in the old familiar way. Alisha's heart lifted. He leaned down to kiss her cheek. "Have you noticed I've trimmed my beard? In honor of the occasion."

"Behave yourself," Alisha scolded, smiling. "It's time to be serious."

"I've never been more serious in my life." And, from the manner in which he repeated his vows, she knew he meant every word.

Then, it was her turn. "Alisha DeFoe, wilt thou have this man to be thy wedded husband, to live together in the holy estate of matrimony? Wilt thou love him, comfort him, honor and keep him, in sickness and in health; and forsaking all others keep thee only unto him, so long as ye both shall live?"

"Oh, yes, I will!"

Alisha's eager response met with muffled laughter and even a sprinkling of applause from some of the former cast members aboard the *Laurel*. She didn't care.

Those precious words had never been so rich with meaning. *Love him, comfort him, honor and keep him, in sickness and in health . . . so long as ye both shall live!* Every day God loaned Zach to her would be a treasure to store up for all the tomorrows of her life.

Suddenly the promise of a very long and happy life with Zach stretched out before her, flowing like the river itself, and Alisha turned to her new husband, lifting her lips to receive his kiss.

ABOUT THE AUTHOR

IRENE B. BRAND is an award-winning inspirational romance writer of eleven romances (both historical and contemporary) and three non-fiction books. Her publishers include Standard Publishing, Fleming H. Revell Company, Thomas Nelson Publishers, Zondervan Publishing House, and Barbour Books. In addition to books, Brand has published devotional literature, teen-age Sunday School curriculum, and articles in several religious and secular publications.

A Master's Degree in History and 23 years of history-teaching experience in West Virginia's public schools have provided valuable background for her historicals. She has also researched for her writing during trips to 22 foreign countries and 46 of the states with her husband, Rod.

After retirement from teaching, Mrs. Brand has devoted herself to full-time writing and to the work of her local church. She also enjoys frequent speaking engagements and keeping in touch with other authors by serving on the staff of writers' conferences.

Forever Romances are inspirational romances designed to bring you a joyful, heart-lifting reading
experience. If you would like more information about
joining our Forever Romance book series, please write
to us:

Guideposts Customer Service
39 Seminary Hill Road
Carmel, NY 10512

Forever Romances are chosen by the same staff that
prepares *Guideposts,* a monthly magazine filled with
true stories of people's adventures in faith. *Guideposts*
is not sold on the newsstand. It's available by subscrip-
tion only. And subscribing is easy. Write to the
address above and you can begin reading *Guideposts*
soon. When you subscribe, each month you can count
on receiving exciting new evidence of God's Presence,
His Guidance and His limitless love for all of us.